"A 'something-for-everyone' book. Turn to any page and get a thought. Read any chapter and get life-changing ideas. Read this book and be enriched for life."

Zig Ziglar, motivational teacher and author of *Over the Top*

"This book will make positive thinking come alive for you in every aspect of your life. Read it; it could be the most important book you have read in a long time."

Ken Blanchard, co-author, *The One Minute Manager*

"Here, once again, is Dr. Schuller at his best with those clear, concise, 'right-on-the-money' words and thoughts that help us mere mortals find out just what it's all about! May be his best book ever!"

Ed McMahon

"You will be all you can be when you read this incredible book. Internalize Dr. Schuller's eight proven principles and you will reinvent yourself for the twenty-first century. Dr. Schuller is the change master who shows us how to turn our mission into a passion, live our dreams instead of chase them, and turn possibilities into certainties."

Dr. Denis Waitley, author of
Empires of the Mind

"Outstanding! Dr. Schuller has done it again. Eight proven principles to live a fuller, happier, and more productive life. This important work shows how to apply God's hope to every situation that life has to offer."

H. Wayne Huizenga,
Huizenga Holdings, Inc.

"Robert Schuller is the dean of the high energy 'can-do' club. *If It's Going to Be, It's Up to Me* is loaded with inspiring stories and useable 'how to' life skills that can lead to a no-limits life. Reading this book is a power transfusion!"

Robert Buford, Chairman of the Board,
Buford Television, Inc.
and author of *Halftime*

IF IT'S GOING TO BE,
IT'S UP TO ME

IF IT'S GOING TO BE, IT'S UP TO ME

The Eight Proven Principles of Possibility Thinking

ROBERT H. SCHULLER

Walker and Company
New York

Published simultaneously in Canada by Thomas Allen & Son Canada, Limited, Markham, Ontario.

All quoted Bible verses are from the *New Possibility Thinkers Bible, New King James Version* (published by Thomas Nelson) and the original *King James Bible*.

Library of Congress Cataloging-in-Publication Data:
Schuller, Robert H.
    If it's going to be, it's up to me : the eight proven principles of possibility thinking / Robert H. Schuller.—1st large print ed.
        p.   cm.
    ISBN 0-8027-2722-0 (pbk.)
    1. Success—Religious aspects—Christianity. 2. Large type books.
I. Title.
[BV4598.3.S384   1997]
248.4—dc21   97–21627
                                                      CIP

First Large Print Edition, 1997
Walker and Company
435 Hudson Street
New York, New York 10014

Printed in the United States of America
10 9 8 7 6 5 4 3 2 1

Dedicated to:

A great American,
A geniune Christian,
A true hero of mine ...
My one and only brother,
Henry Schuller.

CONTENTS

CONTENTS

ACKNOWLEDGMENTS

———✕———

Thank you! Barbara Evans, for taking those yellow pages filled with my handwritten words. Somehow, you were able to read every word, until this entire manuscript was on your word processor.

Thank you! Dr. Arvella Schuller. For twenty-six years, you have produced, edited, and reviewed over 1,400 one-hour television programs for *The Hour of Power*. From this vast resource, you and you only were able to collect and edit so much of the substance that now comes together in this book. When it comes to reading and editing my material, you are the best.

Thank you! Editors and staff of Harper-Collins—Tom Grady, Terri Leonard, Martha Blegen, Ralph Fowler, and Laura Harger. You've been great to work with.

Thank you! Carol Schuller Milner, for allowing me to use your special poem to close this book!

Thank you! Danny Cox, for permission to print your declaration of personal responsibility.

Thank you! To all whose lives have been my inspiration. Their names and their stories are told to inspire all of us to believe that "If it's going to be, it's up to me!"

PREFACE

—⚬—

I am forty years old. I am consumed by a consciousness that overwhelms me. I have to write a book.

It is an awesome awareness that has come to me, not from my undergraduate or postgraduate studies but from experience, which has been my wisest teacher. I am now on to something that has served me, even in these still young years, with stunning success. I have to share these secrets with my friends.

So I write what will become my flagship book, *Move Ahead with Possibility Thinking.* My message? There are really two kinds of persons—"Impossibility Thinkers" and "Possibility Thinkers."

I am totally, completely, absolutely convinced that what I must write is not rhetoric but reality. This book will not be a treatise but a testimony.

DATELINE: 1997 (GARDEN GROVE, CALIFORNIA)

So I wrote the book, that was thirty years ago. That book took a tenacious grip over my thinking that still shapes my dreaming and my doing.

Today I celebrate the thirtieth anniversary of *Move Ahead with Possibility Thinking.* I take the stand now to be judged and cross-examined by my testimony. Have I practiced what I preached for the past three decades? Did my book work for me and for those who listened? Did it continue to work for me, my family, my friends, my ministry, my career? Does possibility thinking still work today? Yes, it works!

The principles of possibility thinking are Classic, Timeless, and Global. For a third of a century I've shared them with literally hundreds of millions of people around the world.

Thousands of doctors, lawyers, corporate chiefs, scientists, and educators tell me that the principles of possibility thinking motivated them through college and postgraduate achievements. "Undergoers" by the hundreds of thousands became "Overcomers" by listening to and learning these principles. Thousands have written me to say that horrific as they were, deaths, divorces, disasters, and depressions did not defeat them.

But mark this well. It is not the book I celebrate today that deserves the credit, nor its author. The glory must go to God, who gave these guidelines for successful and satisfying living in the Holy Bible and in the life of Jesus Christ. I am not the author but a scribe, reporting and recording what I have seen God do to and through people I choose to call Possibility Thinkers.

"If it works, fix it! Make it better."

That's my challenge to myself at the age of seventy. "Why," I ask, "has my lifetime of sharing Possibility Thinking succeeded with so many persons but failed with so many others?" Only at this age and stage of life, having studied failures as well as successes for thirty years, have I come to see how there are **eight proven principles that deliver power into Possibility Thinking.** None of these principles is new or original with me; all have been taught by parents and professors throughout human history.

But what probably has never been done before is the weaving of these eight proven principles into one strong cable.

And they work only when all eight are understood, embraced, and interwoven.

Will this book work for you? Yes. I promise that these power principles will really work if you work them. Your dream of a good life will come true, but it's up to you to make it happen. You must say to yourself, "If it's going to be, it's up to me!"

I have lived a really good life: successful, significant, stimulating, and satisfying. And I now have new twenty-year goals!

So I dare you to listen and learn. I have lived the eight principles you'll read about in this book.

Now it's your turn . . . and you'll discover—faith is a force—not a farce.

INTRODUCTION

1. Who are you? Do you really know?

2. What do you really believe? Is there anything or anyone you'd die for?

3. Where are you coming from? What a collection of memories you have! No, you can't recall them all, but these silent, secret pressures from the past may still be driving you.

4. Where are you headed? Does your life have direction? Purpose? Ambition? Passion?

5. How rich—or poor—are you? What do you own? What do you owe? To whom? Are you satisfied? Should you be? What do you really value?

6. Who are you running with? Are your friends good for you? What's the crowd, culture, community where you've chosen to live? Or didn't you choose? Are you

a product of destiny or a person of decision? Relationships—how do you score?

7. What are your hopes and what are your hurts? Do they control you or do you manage them?

8. What are your successes? Accomplishments? Achievements? Dreams realized? Prayers answered? When, where, and how have you made a positive difference?

9. What are your failures? When and why did you miss the mark? Do you know? Is it important? Any regrets? Disappointments? Can you still put a positive spin on the failures?

10. What's your greatest problem? Some person? Your position? Or are you your biggest problem? Why? Apathy or ignorance? Are you living with decisions you've made or failed to make? What decisive changes could you make that would correct, improve, or expand the consequences you're reaping today?

11. Your emotions—are they your friends? Or foes? Are you in touch with them? What would move you to tears? Happy tears? Or sweet sad tears? What feel-

ings have you enjoyed the most? What powerful emotions have you never experienced? Why not? Are you in a rut? Do you dare to face the possibility of strange and foreign feelings?

12. Finally, are you alive? Do you have dreams still unfulfilled? Are these positive opportunities still within your unlived tomorrows? What persons, projects, passions, and performances would you pursue if you knew you wouldn't fail? What grand, good, and glorious impossibilities would you go after if you could see them not as impossibilities but as eventual achievements—if?—with?—when?—after?

So now—what do you really want before you pack your suitcase, before your curtain drops? Before you check out—check in!

Be alert! Wake up! A new dream will emerge from the shadows of yesterday and today to become a beautiful, bright light on your tomorrows!

Be open and receptive to a new vision of a new you.

There's a new life, a new you, a beautiful future waiting to happen all around you.

You've never experienced tomorrow before. There's something bright and beautiful out there through possibility thinking! If you can dream it, you can do it!

Let me be your tour guide.

I'm in the exciting business of researching, discovering, developing, and achieving untouched, untapped, and unexplored human potential.

I've interviewed and count as my friends the poor, the middle class, and the rich. I sit on the board of the Horatio Alger Association, which is an organization made up of the most successful high achievers, all of whom started with nothing!

Now I want you to meet my friends in these pages. You'll learn success secrets from them. I met them on the street, through other friends, and through letters—millions of letters over the past twenty years! I'm not talking just about persons born with a silver spoon in their mouth. I'm talking about people just like you!

I'm not a psychologist; I'm not a commercial motivator; I'm not a plagiarist of positive promotional slogans. I've written thirty books on this specialized subject of success and failure. I speak to millions of people each week, crossing countries, cultures, philosophies, and religions on the longest-running and most widely viewed television program ever aired. And I offer to persons solid, sensible faith and hope.

Many—yes, tens of thousands—have overcome every imaginable human hardship, struggle, horror, and pain! I've seen them become dreamers of a new dream. I've seen them step into the fantastic world of possibility thinking. I've walked with them through cancer, bankruptcy, depression, and failure. I've watched as they've gone on to dream a new dream, and I've seen them make that dream happen!

Trust me!

Step with me into an exciting new world you've never known before.

Join me on a trip I know well. Yes, I have a new dream—the dream is you! If your dream is going to come true, it's up to you. Yes, this book is all about your responsibility as you face your possibility.

Here's how you'll make it happen. Start here and now, by seeing, seizing, and saying:

—⚬—

If it's going to be, It's up to me!

—⚬—

Make your thinking big enough for God to fit in.

"Make it simple and make it work," you respond. I accept your challenge.

From all of the positive people I've met, all the books I've written and read, all the seminars and success lectures I've been a part of over the past forty years, I can sum up the eight principles of powerful possibility thinking in eight rhyming lines:

Ode to Sweet and Satisfying Success

Possibilities must be weighed.
Priorities must be swayed.
Plans must be laid.
Commitments must be made.
The price must be paid.
The timing may be delayed.
The course must be stayed.
And the trumpets will be played.

I'm often asked, "Dr. Schuller, what in your opinion is the most helpful book that you've ever written?"

I usually answer, "My last one."

But if you ask me today, I have a new answer: "My next one."

So here it is! Dedicated to you!

I don't want you to fail. I want to help you succeed as you never have before!

Simply read this next sentence out loud: "If it's going to be, it's up to me!"

The next century—Century 21—will belong first and foremost to a new mental breed of humans driven by a strong, sensitive, spiritual individualism.

That's where it's at today. Get with it! Let's move up and ahead with the power of possibility thinking.

———⚒———

Say it again.
Louder! Stronger! . . .
"If it's going to be,
it's up to me!"

———⚒———

There's only one person on earth who can dream your dreams. That person is you!

There's only one person alive who can kill that dream. That person is you!

There's only one person who can decide to make your dream come true. That person is you!

The Dream of Doing leads to success. The Dream of Being leads to significance.

Make this profound decision now: decide that you won't be a product, a computer, or a puppet—but a person! "If it's going to be, it's up to me."

I dare you to read this book. I dare you to read all eight chapters.

I dare you to grasp and grip the eight non-negotiable, proven principles that must be perceived, then personally applied in your personality, to release the power of possibility thinking.

I guarantee this message! I promise you that if you absorb and apply all eight principles, you'll discover this uncompromising formula for personal achievement:

—⟋⟋⟍—

Possibility + Responsibility = Success

—⟋⟋⟍—

IF IT'S GOING TO BE, IT'S UP TO ME

I

POSSIBILITIES
MUST BE WEIGHED

—⟁—

I'm often asked, "What are the most impressive, informative, and inspirational books you've ever read?" and "What books have you been reading this year?" I answer both questions in one word: "Persons." I watch people. I listen to them. I learn from them. In doing so, I'm reading the books that haven't been written yet. I "read" people's words and their work, their play and their prayer. I "read" their hurts and their hopes, their successes and their failures, their dreams and their disappointments, their sin and their salvation. I "read" them as I listen to them while we visit and have fellowship; while they deliberate, debate, or dictate. Their life's story is unfolded in the news on television, in newspapers, in journals, in magazines.

Every person is an open book. What laboratories in living they all are! Winners and losers. Dreamers and doers. Some are "make it happen" people; some are "waiting for others to make it happen" people. I look at them. I listen to them. I pray for the wisdom to hear what they can teach by their success and their failure. What fascinating and fruitful reading is to be had in the people we meet, the ones we live with! We can read history, anthropology, sociology, psychology, religion, politics, art, and architecture. Finance, business, management—it's all there! Even quiet people are books to read. Freudian slips are all around us—in everybody!

What have I learned from reading all of the books put before me—printed and unprinted? That life is made up of this basic scientific reality: possibility thinking versus impossibility thinking. All living people expose an unpublished autobiography. Study these unfinished books. Ask yourself, "When and where did these people 'make it'—or 'miss it'?"

You'll find that the answer to that question always depends on how they managed the positive opportunities to become the persons they were designed and destined by God to be.

S ome

positive

possibilities

just come

out of

the blue.

POSSIBILITIES:
LIFE IS LOADED WITH THEM

When, where, and how do people see the possibilities?

In needs that must be filled. . . . In challenges that inspire you to do and be more than you ever imagined. . . . In problems waiting to be solved. . . . In pain that cries out for help. . . . In joys and sorrows that, when wonderfully and wisely shared, become lifesaving forces and sources to encourage someone who "reads the story."

Gaby Kennard was the first Australian woman to fly around the world, solo, in a single-engine Piper Saratoga. It was a heroic flight. She was faced with instrument malfunction before she left Australia. She was robbed of precious survival gear. And in high winds, close to running out of fuel, she was forced to make an emergency landing at a high-security military airfield. These are just a few of the serious challenges she faced, but she followed her dream in spite of them. She conquered her challenges and didn't surrender to negative thoughts. After ninety-nine days of flying, she reached her final destination and accomplished her goal.

As a little kid, Gaby had always dreamed of

flying, and as soon as she was old enough, she learned to fly. But simply piloting a plane wasn't enough. She was thirty-three when an exciting possibility gripped her: "Someday I'm going to fly around the world!" she said to herself. "Alone!"

Gaby had a lot of difficulties to overcome even before she took off. She didn't have an airplane, for example, nor did she have any money. The one thing she did own was her house. She refinanced that to buy a plane but still needed financial support to pay for fuel and for the modifications that she needed to make the plane fit for the long journey she dreamed of. Slowly the money came in.

While she waited and worked, Gaby had to believe passionately in herself and in her dream. She had to overcome her own negativity. "I can't do it," she would tell herself periodically. But then the dream would pull her on. She also faced the negativity of other people: "What qualifies you to do this?" people demanded. "How do you think you're going to pull this off? You're irresponsible to even think about it!"

So, as Gaby told our *Hour of Power* audience, "There was a little crowd to see me off on my round-the-world trip, but there was a big crowd when I got back."

Gaby left Sidney via New Guinea and flew across the ocean to Hawaii; from there she flew to the continental United States, commemorating Amelia Earhart's attempt to fly around the world in 1937. Gaby described her difficult flight:

"I was discouraged many times. I went through storms. Then—worst of all—I had engine failure, five times, on the longest leg, the one between Hawaii and Oakland, California. I had a problem with my fuel selector valve. Those were the scariest moments of my life, but I made it. I actually solved the problems, and I made it to California. But when I got to California, I was terribly afraid to take off again. I attempted to take off three times, the perspiration pouring off my face. And then on the third failed attempt to take off, I was so terrified that I went into the airport office at the Oakland airport. Who should happen to be on the television screen but Dr. Schuller. And you said to me, 'To realize your dream, you must break through your barriers of fear.' Of course, I thought you were speaking to me personally!

"When I was preparing for this flight, two individual people gave me a little plaque with your words, 'If you can dream it, you can do it.' Now you were saying to me, via television, 'You must break through your barriers of fear if you're to realize your dream.' So I said, 'Right. I'll do it, Dr. Schuller!'

"So I got in my little airplane—the perspiration still dripping down. I was shaking as I pushed my throttle forward, forcing my little plane down the runway and taking off. When I got to about a thousand feet above ground, I thought, 'I've done it! I've broken through my barrier of fear!'"

So Gaby continued across the United States to South America, over the Amazon jungles to Africa, across the Middle East to India, and then across Thailand and back to Australia, where there was a big crowd to welcome her home.

In reflecting on that adventure, Gaby said, "I learned a lot of big lessons. It was like a concentrated lifetime in ninety-nine days. I learned to take responsibility for myself. Not to ever think, 'I'm a victim.' I have a good capacity to reason; not only that, I have a huge amount of help that I can draw on apart from myself. In other words, we all have great resources within ourselves that we don't realize. And it wasn't only coming from inside me; it was coming from the outside as well. I had a lot of support from the universe and God. There were people who really cared for me. We all have this immense ability to do what we want! We can achieve anything. It's not always easy, but we can."

Gaby learned through her personal experience the absolute truth of this one line, which sums up all success slogans in a single sentence: "If it's going to be, it's up to me!"

I won my marks in college in speaking, oratory, and debate. I was honored to be elected into the National Honorary Forensic Fraternity, Pi Kappa Delta. How I treasured the golden key I was given! But I got an F in English. The professor, who knew me, said, "Robert, focus on speaking and forget writing." So, from an expert, I concluded that I'd never be an author. I might have lived my whole life under that negative judgment except for a possibility that came out of the blue.

I was assigned by my denomination to organize a church in a new suburb in Southern California. At its inception, it had only four members: myself, Arvella (my wife), Sheila (my four-year-old daughter), and Robert Anthony (my six-month-old son). I needed to let the community know who I was and what I was doing. I needed good publicity, so I went to the largest newspaper in town to find out what it would cost to run an ad announcing my new church. I wasn't at all sure I could afford paid advertising on my very limited budget.

The person who helped me said, "While you're here, let me introduce you to the owner and publisher, Mr. R. C. Hoiles. He's a powerful man in this community. He's not religious, and he's not a professing believer, but he's a big promoter of the Ten Commandments." We walked down the hall and through his open door, and there he sat behind his desk. He was reading the new day's edition of his daily paper, the *Santa Ana Register*—today known as the *Orange County Register.*

My escort said, "Mr. Hoiles, may I introduce a minister who's moved in to start a new church?"

Hoiles's welcome was polite but lacked a warm enthusiasm.

"What church do you belong to?" I asked.

"I don't belong to any church, Reverend. I have problems with organized religion." Then he threw me a question: "Do you believe in the Ten Commandments, Reverend? It seems preachers don't preach on them anymore. We need to learn morality—don't lie, don't steal, don't kill—you know!" He was blunt and to the point.

"Oh, yes, sir—I agree with you."

His eyes burned through me as he searched my soul. Then he hit me with one of the greatest possibilities I've ever been offered by anyone, anytime, anywhere in my career.

"You preach a sermon on each of the Ten Commandments, Reverend, and I'll publish them all—word for word in my newspaper. I won't pay you a dime, but I'll publish them—free! Make them good, and it'll be the best and cheapest publicity this paper can give you."

Instantly I saw and seized the possibility. After we shook hands, I went home and planned my next ten sermons. Although I wondered whether I could write them out well enough to be in public print, I didn't care that I wasn't a "writer." I was desperately in need of exposure.

I wrote the first sermon out word for word. I rewrote it. I revised it. I added verbs, adjectives, and adverbs. Without knowing much about composition, I simply wrote sentences that to my mind were simple, understandable, and sensible. I turned it in to Mr. Hoiles.

Without reading it, he promised, "I'll publish it—exactly as you wrote it, without editorial corrections or comments." Then he added this disclaimer. "I'll print this, but only on one condition."

"What's that?" I asked.

"That you promise you'll give me nine more in the next nine weeks. I'll print one a week for the next ten weeks."

I promised. I delivered. He printed. When the ten weeks were past, I reread all of the ten messages—and I was impressed! I typed a title page, "God's Way to the Good Life," and boldly—impertinently—sent the sermons to Wm. Eerdman's Publishing Company in Grand Rapids, Michigan. After all, I owned several books of sermons by ministers published by that company. In only a few weeks I got a promise from them to publish my "book." A contract was enclosed. I signed it. Eerdman's made money on it and wanted me to write another book of sermons on the twenty-third psalm. Suddenly I was on my way to becoming a published writer, even though I was nobody as an author.

Thirty years ago—some eight years after the publication of my first book—I would write a serious work, *Move Ahead with Possibility Thinking*. I thought I had it made by then. But not quite! I wasn't known nationally. And this wasn't the kind of a book that publishers like Eerdman's were interested in. Publisher after publisher rejected it.

Again and again the manuscript was returned to me with the large letters REJECTED stamped across the first page. But I believed in that book with all my heart. Finally I sent the manuscript to Doubleday in New York—and it was accepted! Norman Vincent Peale read it and loved it. He even wrote a glowing foreword. That book was published and became a best-seller. The rest is history. Today countless copies of my books are in print around the world. And twenty-five years after its publication, *Move Ahead with Possibility Thinking* was translated into Chinese. That translation became a best-seller as well, with over a million and a half copies sold to would-be entrepreneurs in the new China.

Thank you, Mr. R. C. Hoiles and the *Orange County Register!* You handed me a possibility that academic experts had led me to believe was an impossibility!

See and seize the possibilities within yourself!

In the Talmud, Hillel is recorded as saying,

If I am not for myself who will be?
If I am only for myself—what am I?

Now this book is dedicated to you! Your happiness. Your success. Your fulfillment. Your joy!

Jesus Christ predicted—no, promised—that within each and every human being fantastic potential is waiting to be discovered and developed.

He proclaimed these powerful words: "The Kingdom of God is within you" (Luke 17:21). This means that there's an Eternal Creative Force within you. Mind and matter are alive with an energy that can be tapped and channeled to joyful creativity. See and seize it in science, in art and literature, in interpersonal relationships, in positive emotional power.

The power that we call God is designed to

flow into, and through, the personalities and personal spiritual powers of human beings. When this dynamic divine energy is ignited within the human personality, the creative energy of the eternal God comes alive within us and we begin to experience and express phenomenal achievements; we begin to make a beautiful difference in our world. Then we become truly wonderful—yes, full of wonder—persons. "I wonder how she did it?" "I wonder how he made it?" That's living in the Kingdom of God.

My friend Chuck Taylor has impacted the world. There isn't a satellite in space, over the free world, that his company doesn't have parts on. He was the only son of a great military commander who was killed on Corregidor. With his father's death, Charles became the ten-year-old head of his household, helping his mother and two sisters. He went to the Naval Academy, graduated with distinction, and was off on a remarkable career—a career that would take him into high-tech specialized creativity. The first company Chuck started was a success primarily due to the investors. Then he took the company public and merged with other small companies. His enlarged company was bought out by a still larger company that "let Chuck go." So, at the age of forty, he was out of a job. He had a wife, house payments, three children. And he also had a lot of faith and positive thoughts. Depressed? No way! He simply started a new company. He believed that everything happens for the best. And it certainly did for him. He made several proposals and designs for NASA's Viking Program, which landed two space probes on Mars. National space experts were impressed enough to come down and survey Chuck's new company and audit what he and his people were doing.

"They sent more people down to the company than I employed," Chuck told me. "We didn't have any heritage, but we had a lot of ideas and a lot of faith. They finally accepted our ideas. By the time the Viking Program was over—which was a very, very successful project—we had forty-four different products on that mission.

"During the business day it's very hectic, as you can imagine, so I don't get many ideas during the day. We brainstorm some thoughts, but it's not until I go to bed at night and I pray every evening that creative ideas come to me. I always have a Dictaphone by my side. When I awaken early in the morning or sometimes during the middle of the night, I'll write down or jot down or record these ideas. My secretary dreads long weekends!"

This is how God lives within us and leads us with creative ideas. He creates different people, mixes genes and chromosomes, creates unique creatures with different gifts—intellectual, emotional, and creative. In the Bible we read, "And My thoughts are higher than your thoughts" (Isaiah 55:9).

You—yes, you and every other human being—are designed with an emotional consciousness that can connect with the higher thoughts of God. At night, the Creator is free to get into your head with creativity. He doesn't have to interrupt the television, the radio, the fax machine, or other people.

One morning, Chuck Taylor was watching television and saw what the whole nation saw: a terrible disaster within our space-shuttle program. The seven astronauts aboard the *Challenger* had been killed—the greatest tragedy in space. Chuck Taylor instantly suspected what had gone wrong. Soon the problem was identified, and his suspicion was confirmed: an O-ring had become too cold, lost some resiliency, and failed.

And Chuck knew that he had a solution to the tragic problem. He understood the magnitude of the space program and the space shuttle. He knew that on liftoff the shuttle weighed four million, three hundred thousand pounds. The solid rocket boosters that put it into orbit produce thirty-six million horsepower, burning solid rocket fuel at the rate of nine tons per second. That's four swimming pools of fuel every minute to propel that mission. It would be an awesome assignment.

But Chuck told me what happened next: "I was so confident of an idea that I had that would correct the O-ring problem. Of the seventeen other leading companies that were brought to NASA, I was probably the smallest. They said they were going to select only one company and only one solution. The way it was said, my heart sank. I was so confident and I had so much faith in what I had proposed. When the head of NASA put his hand out to shake mine, I was almost reluctant to shake it. He said, 'By the way, the company and the solution that we've selected is you, Tayco Engineering.' Then he looked down at our handshake and said, 'This is your authority to get started now.' Since that time we've had forty-two successful space flights."

But one of the most rewarding challenges that Chuck Taylor has enjoyed is contributing to the development of a cochlear implant for the profoundly deaf for the House Ear Institute.

The development of the cochlear implant by Dr. William and Dr. Howard House was dependent on a technique that Chuck had developed for NASA: welding extremely fine wire to a terminal—wire one-fourth the diameter of a human hair, so small you can't see it except under a microscope. That technology was necessary to complete the development of the world's first cochlear implant. "I never invoiced them for that cost," Chuck told me, "but I was paid more than money could ever begin to pay me. I witnessed the first child given a cochlear implant hearing for the very first time.

"We were watching through one-way glass, so the child couldn't see us. Everybody was watching him as he played with some blocks. Then they sent the first sound into the room that this child had ever heard. He looked up, startled, and there wasn't a dry eye among us. It was truly wonderful."

That's Chuck Taylor's story. What a special gift to the world God has given to us through Chuck's talents and dedicated spirit! He's fulfilling the prediction and promise that Jesus Christ made: "You are the salt of the earth" (Matthew 5:13).

Salt adds spice to the taste. Salt replaces boredom with excitement. You become the subtle and sensational force that brings fresh flavor and delightful fragrance into the drab, dreary, mental climate around you. And salt preserves as well. Your personality restores the joy of living to human existence and endurance.

"You are the light of the world" (Matthew 5:14), Jesus added. Yes, people who are spiritually and emotionally connected to the Eternal Creative Force discover their powerful potential as a creative personality and win the big prize in living. They become—yes, you become—a light in darkness. Light? Yes, an inspiration to your friends, neighbors, family, and community. You become a "light-turned-on person."

You become a cheerful light that replaces gloom with gladness. What a difference you make when your life becomes a light turned on!

Real estate people have learned that to succeed in the sale of a house, they need to turn on the lights in every room before an interested customer steps inside. Even on a bright, sunny day, even in a home with many windows, the turned-on lights add warmth and cheer, leaving no gloomy corners. Yes, you become a cheerful personality who radiates hope.

You become a guiding light. "If he could do

it—maybe I can too." Your achievements become the creative inspirational light igniting the glow of hope in the drab, dark, dreary, discouraged minds of those who see your story lived out for all the world to read. The message you send is sincere and clear:

"I came from nowhere and went somewhere!"

"I was a nobody—and I really became a somebody!"

"I'm a bright light in a dark world!"

You can become that kind of inspiring person. You're the salt of the earth. You're the light of the world. What a stunning life-view is laid out before you—here! Now!

One of the most awesome experiences I ever lived through happened in the heat of the Cold War, when America and the free world were in a terribly dangerous and costly confrontation with the Soviet Union and the dictatorial system of Communism. Under Stalin, several Eastern European countries had been overrun by Soviet invaders pursuing Hitler. When Germany was defeated, Moscow kept its power and presence in these small, independent nations, placing puppet leaders over each one. Each country was forced to abandon its economic, religious, and institutional freedom to the new philosophy of Communism. When Hungary resisted, revolting against the invasive, oppressive Soviet domination and declaring her intention to be free, overnight the mighty Soviet military machine rolled in on highways and railways to crush the revolution. The Hungarian uprising was quickly squelched. Neighboring Czechoslovakia noticed and trembled.

Now, some years later, my traveling companion and I were in the Soviet Union. We had completed our mission in an atmosphere of tension. We couldn't wait to return to freedom in Austria. Our exit would be by train from Lvov in the Ukraine to Vienna in Austria. At the train station in Lvov, Soviet soldiers were everywhere. Anxiously, we longed for Vienna, our gateway to freedom.

My companion and I boarded the long passenger train and were led to our tiny compartment. It would be a long ride through both darkness and daylight, so we settled in for the long haul. Suddenly, with no warning announcement, we were jolted awake. It was daylight now. Our door was slammed open by a Soviet soldier, red stars on both lapels of his green jacket. He spoke no English, but in an angry tone and with unmistakable gestures, he made it clear that we had to get up, go out the door, march down the narrow hall, and get off the train—which by now had stopped. We stepped down the steel steps leading to a wide cement street running along the rails. Looking in both directions, we could see people getting off every one of the probably thirty or more passenger cars. It was a total evacuation, from the locomotive to the last car. A parade of officials in a strange uniform—not Soviet—were herding the passengers back and away from the train, as if it were about to blow up.

Suddenly, a parade of the strangest-looking vehicles appeared at the locomotive end. What were they? Each one was a low-profile four-wheeler carrying a huge jack. Passengers moved back farther from the cars to make space for the parade. One vehicle was moved to each passenger car. In a matter of only minutes, these machines were in place. From every jack, two "arms" were extended out, reaching underneath the railroad cars.

An American professor who had made this trip before approached us and explained: "You'll see something unusual here! We're on the border just inside Czechoslovakia. This nation has made sure Soviet trains will never invade her land by building narrow railroad tracks throughout the country. These jacks you see will raise all of the train cars so that the Soviet wheels can be removed and rolled back into the Soviet Union."

I watched as the jacks slowly raised all of the cars on our long passenger train three, four, five feet. Now the entire train of cars was suspended in air, the wheels remaining on the track below! Then all of the abandoned Soviet wheels were pushed one against another, like dominoes, until they were all propelled back into the Soviet Union on the wider track on which they'd just come. "Look," our new acquaintance said, pointing to the track cleared of all wheels. "Now you can see the second track—inside the wide abandoned rails. This narrow track continues into Czechoslovakia. In a moment—look west—you'll see the wheels of freedom. They'll roll these down and under every passenger car. Here they come!" From the far Czechoslovakia end came another parade of wheels—narrower this time, to fit the narrower inside track of rails. The jacked-up passenger cars were all high enough for those Czech wheels to slide underneath.

In an amazingly brief time the new wheels were in place under each car. Then, with a loud hum, the huge jacks began to move again, and the entire passenger train—all thirty-plus cars still connected together, stretching perhaps a quarter-mile—was lowered onto its new wheels on the inside track. If and when Czechoslovakia decided to throw off their Russian yoke, no trains loaded with soldiers would be able to roll into their free land. The officials waved the parade of passengers back onto the train. We were fitted to enter Freedom's Land. We were really on a new track! A narrower track of success!

Jesus Christ, the Master Teacher, wisely shared this principle two thousand years ago: "Wide is the road that leads to destruction and many are walking that dismal trail. But narrow is the way that leads to life and few there are that find it" (Matthew 7:13, 14).

What's Jesus really saying? There are two tracks we can take.

The broad track, which leads to final futility, folly, and failure, is the track I call impossibility thinking. Its popular appeal exploits the fears and inferiority complexes of insecure humans. "You can't do it." "You're too young [or too old]." "You don't have the money, the organization, the rich friends, the education, the talent or skill, or the impressive record in school and society to be a real success." "Face it," the negative cultural exploiters of the "have-nots" declare: "You don't have the color, culture, credentials, or connections to make it in today's world." They say, "Accept your fate, which is to live your insignificant life on a low-potential level." "Bury your beautiful—but impossible—dreams." "Settle for the stimulation you can buy in a bag, a bottle, a bed, or a bar!" "Go with the easy flow."

This is the broad way. You can choose to surrender leadership over your destiny to fears, to negative-thinking "friends" and family, to social and political forces that would intimidate and manipulate you until you've surrendered your personal potential, becoming only a puppet, a product, or a possession someone owns and uses for his or her own end.

Then there's the narrow way. It's another option. It too is yours to choose. But it isn't just another variation of the broad way. It's a totally alternative decision. I call it possibility thinking. It's a competing, challenging, and truly creative option.

Yes, there are two tracks you can take. It's your choice. You're free to decide.

What a narrow way possibility thinking is! "I may not have the money—but I can make a little, save a little, earn more, and reach my goal anyway!"

"I may not have the training, the education, or the intelligence, but I've got something more important than a high IQ. I've got a high EQ—emotional quotient! A high EQ is a heart that has strong faith, unquenchable hope, and passionate love. Listen to the high-EQ person: I can get smart, or meet and hire people who are smarter than I am! I can choose any dream I want—and go for it."

Two tracks. One is narrow—that's the high-EQ route. One is broad—that's the low-EQ route. You may choose which path to take: impossibility thinking or possibility thinking!

Broad is the road that leads to failure and futility. Narrow is the way that leads to success and achievement. Attack your impossibility complex and attach yourself to possibility thinkers!

OBSTACLES: HOW TO SURMOUNT THEM

Why do most people choose the wide track of negative impossibility thinking? What motivates them to take the path that leads them away from the really big prizes? Prizes such as these:

• Prosperity instead of poverty

- Humble pride instead of low self-esteem
- Fulfillment instead of emptiness

What holds people back from freely choosing a positive attitude toward positive possibilities? What keeps a person locked into mental thinking that promises no real progress? Two words to sum it up: Intimidation! Manipulation! I've spent a lifetime as a counselor and a motivator, and I can sum up the major reasons persons loaded with potential never see or seize their opportunities: provincialism, paternalism, prejudice, power circles, poverty, prosperity, and problems. I can also offer some rules that will help you escape these problems. Let's look at each rule in turn.

Rule 1

BREAK FREE FROM THE INVISIBLE PERSONS AND POWERS OF NEGATIVE PROVINCIALISM

The term provincialism comes from the word province—that is, territory—and means "limited in outlook." Provincialism can infect individualism. A child raised in a small-thinking family, school, or community will tend to become a person of limited vision. Negative-thinking communities and cultures and creeds can intimidate the would-be visionary with the fear of criticism and ridicule on the part of those who've never dared to "make a break for it." Those people—the majority—will be slow to encourage the young dreamer of great dreams. Broad is the way that leads to the destruction of daring dreamers.

One of the reasons the United States of America has shattered all national success records in human history is that we were founded by dreamers of great dreams—inspired and inspiring immigrants who dared to leave home and turn their backs on family and relatives to find a better life for their children. They broke free from the invisible prison that provincialism can impose. Provincialism is often controlled by tyrannical traditions. Provincialism intimidates—and thereby manipulates—the would-be explorer and adventurer.

"My friends said, 'You can't do it! Face it: your family isn't in that class!' My family said, 'Nobody in our community or in our family ever goes to the university!'" The young girl who was speaking to me was one of the eighty-nine graduating high school seniors who were carefully selected by the Horatio Alger Association. We brought them to our annual meeting in Washington, D.C. All were poor. That was a given. No rich kids were eligible. The Horatio Alger Association is made up of extremely successful leaders who started in poverty and overcame huge challenges to rise to the top of the ladder in their profession and career.

I listened to her, enthralled, as she continued: "I was raised in this pocket of Hispanic poverty. Everybody who was born there died there—or went to jail. People who left were running away from something bad. They weren't running to something good. Nobody in our barrio ever encouraged anyone to go somewhere and be somebody. My mother ran away from home. My dad was alcoholic. Both of them were on drugs. Since the age of twelve, I've had to earn my own money for my food, clothes, shelter. I started out earning dollars baby-sitting. Now I've graduated from high school at the top of my class. And with the scholarship I've won from the Horatio Alger members, I'm going to the university and I'm going to be somebody. I'm going to be the first person in my family and one of the first persons in my community to get a college degree!"

She did it! She got off the broad way that leads to destruction. She's on the narrow way—faith-filled and focused on life!

"How did you ever get the vision—the dream—living where you lived?" I asked. I wondered how a girl with her background could see the possibilities.

"Well, there was this family that ran a store," she explained. "Compared to most of us, who were really poor—well, they were rich. One day the lady in the store said, 'I like you. How would you like to baby-sit for my little girl tonight? My husband and I want to go to a movie. We'll pay you a dollar.' A whole dollar! I did it. It was the first time in my life I held a dollar bill that was all mine in my hand! They liked me. I became their regular baby-sitter. I saved the money to buy food. And one day I had enough money to even buy a pair of nice used jeans in a mission store. Then one day this lady asked me, 'Where do you plan to live all your life? What do you want to be? You could buy this store someday. Or you could go to school and become a nurse or a doctor.'

"The store owner was really serious! She and I laughed, but that's where I began to dream that a beautiful life and future were possible if I just believed in myself. 'Never forget,' the lady said, 'you can go anywhere and be anything you want to be, Suzanne.'"

This young woman positively twinkled as

she shared the birth of positive possibilities in her thinking. She exuded energy. "But!"—the young girl now raised her voice, locked her eyes with mine, touched the top of my right hand, and said—"Dr. Schuller, it was God who came into my life and gave me faith in Jesus and in myself! I was invited to a small Sunday School, where I became a believer in God. And we had to memorize Bible verses. One I was assigned has become the greatest line I've ever lived by. It's 'I can do all things through Christ who strengthens me'" (Philippians 4:13).

Tears welled up in her eyes as she smiled and confessed, "Life has been hard for me. As I told you, ever since I was twelve years old, I've had to earn my own bread, clothes, and shelter. And I guess life will always be hard, because I've set goals that I know aren't going to be easy. But every night I pray before I fall asleep, and when I wake up, I've got new strength. I wouldn't trade my life for anything."

If it's going to be, it's up to me.

How do you weigh the possibilities? Begin by breaking free from negative provincialism.

Be bold!

Courage isn't

feeling free

from fear;

courage is

facing fears

you feel!

Rule 2

BREAK FREE FROM PATERNALISM

The narrow road requires that we break free from paternalism—that safe, comfortable, but deceptive attitude.

The word paternalism comes from the root noun pater, which means "father." Paternalism can be an invisible prison—trapping fearful persons and preventing them from seeing, sensing, sizing up, and seizing the possibilities in their life. Paternalism assumes that one or more of the following—a good religion with a heavenly Father, good politics with a protective government, or a good society made up of wealthy philanthropists—have an obligation to fill the good-father role and provide for all of our needs.

Paternalism is the mental attitude that "father will provide." And good fathers do. Their children grow up well served and amply provided for, expecting that society is made up of good people by whom they can expect to be cared for. A famous philanthropist who started in poverty and became very successful earned the reputation for overcoming many obstacles. As he neared the end of his life, he was asked, "What's the hardest job you've ever faced in life?" His answer:

"Learning how to help family and friends without doing them more harm than good."

Paternalism. Now you can see why many wealthy fathers who started from scratch to make their fortune buy their children the expensive toys they themselves never had. "I don't want my kids to go through what I went through," they say protectively. And those children are never challenged to discover and develop their own potential. By contrast, now you can see how we must applaud the children of successful parents who on their own expand their inheritance daringly, ambitiously, and aggressively.

Mrs. Schuller and I—successful in our life's work, despite challenges, problems, mountains, and obstacles—knew that there was one all-important lesson each of our five children must learn. That lesson is the title of this book! Each child would have to set a goal that could release exciting possibilities into his or her imagination—a goal made by the child alone, without Dad's help. So we set the law down firmly in our family: (1) Each child, upon graduation from high school, would have to go to college and complete that education with a bachelor of arts degree or its equal. (2) The children could pick the school of their choice, but it had to be a college far enough from our home that they'd be separated from their father and their mother. (3) I'd pay for their food, lodging, and tuition, but they'd have to choose their courses and pass them with honorable grades— all of which they knew was a challenge I couldn't and wouldn't help with. Paternalism was now out. Personal responsibility—possibility-thinking individualism —was in.

How do good people help those who need help without holding them back from making life's most important discovery: "I'm somebody! I can do it"? As a father, I'll never— never—forget the morning I drove my firstborn child, Sheila, to the airport when she left home for college. Noticing my misty eyes as I drove on the busy freeway, she saved the day.

"Dad! Don't cry. I memorized those special words you gave me for this moment." Her eyes, too, were filled with tears. Her lips moved confidently, though, and the poetry came out without faltering:

"Grieve not for me
who am about to start
a new adventure.
Eager I stand and ready to depart.
Me and my reckless
Pioneering heart."

She was well on her way, escaping from the possibility of being imprisoned by a beautiful, loving, protective—but ultimately destructive—paternalism. She was learning her biggest and best lesson: "If it's going to be, it's up to me!" All five of our children would leave home after high school to go to college, except for our daughter Carol, who chose a different, equally challenging route.

After the amputation of her left leg in a motorcycle accident, Carol needed to learn how to be active again, so she elected to attend a handicapped ski program on her own in Winter Park, Colorado. One of the hardest jobs her good father has ever had was to take this seventeen-year-old daughter to the airport—with her crutches, a spare prosthesis, and her skis. She'd already spent three years painfully recovering from her near-fatal motorcycle accident; now she saw exciting possibilities in this new sport: handicapped skiing. "Dad, I'd like to really go for it! I'm sure I can make the Handicapped Olympics! But I need to get into the best training program, and that's in Colorado."

Her mother and I knew immediately that she could live with an amputated leg, but she'd never live with an amputated spirit. We had to let her go! She had to live away from her mother and father, who'd been with her every day for seven months in the hospital and many additional months at home. Now we saw her onto the plane. She was leaving home, alone. It's painful for a good father and mother to resist yielding to the heart-rending call to become paternalistic parents. How do you help a hurting person without amputating her spirit from her dream? Inflicting added injuries to her fragile, wounded, and very vulnerable person?

Carol had to say goodbye to her father and mother in order to say hello to her future. Of course, we cried at the airport! She'd have to do for herself—alone—what doctors, nurses, and her parents had been doing for her for the past three years. She'd live alone in a small apartment almost half a nation away from home, cooking her meals, nursing her still-healing stump. Setting her alarm to rise early and spend hours training, day after day, week after week, month after month.

Would she discover and develop her untapped human potential and win the big prize—self-reliance? Would the adventure in competitive skiing be better for her than a first year in college? We weighed that possibility carefully and prayerfully! The decision she made—with our still-bleeding hearts supporting her—was beyond doubt the best decision. She would go on to win many silver and gold medals, but her greatest medal wasn't one that would be slipped around her neck at a national competition. Instead, invisibly inscribed with these words—"If it's going to be, it's up to me!"—it was one she wore around her heart.

So all of our five children left home in search of possibilities after high school! "Didn't your children ever rebel and want to leave home?" we're often asked. The answer: "No—they didn't have a chance! We sent them away before they wanted to go away!" They were sent to a positive place, in a possibility-pregnant environment, as soon as they could venture out and discover who they really were meant by God to be and to become.

I was one of eighty persons to attend one of the most illuminating meetings of the century. President George Bush decided to reveal and record for history the true picture of how the Cold War ended in peace without a third world war. Early in 1995, in a twenty-four-hour retreat at a Colorado get-away, he called together those leaders who had brought the dangerous Cold War to a peaceful end—representatives of five major nations that had confronted each other for decades. He invited Brian Mulroney from Canada, Margaret Thatcher from England, François Mitterand from France, and Mikhail Gorbachev from the former Soviet Union, while he, George Bush, represented America. These five former heads of state sat in small armchairs on an open stage to share honestly what happened, when, and why, to bring this horrendous age to a peaceful ending.

All alone on stage, these men and women who had been leaders of the Cold War world during the most crisis-filled years of the twentieth century faced each other openly and honestly hour after hour, without staff assistants to guide their answers.

At one point in their dialogue, George Bush turned to Margaret Thatcher and said, "The first crack in the Iron Curtain happened—I think we all agree—when you met Mikhail Gorbachev, the new Soviet president, on his first visit to England. When he left, you told the world, 'I think we can work with this man.' This was a historic breakthrough—for you, a strong anti-Communist, to predict this positive possibility. What caused you to change your thinking?"

"Well, when Mr. Gorbachev agreed to come to London, I asked myself, 'Where should I receive him? At my office in London?' Then I got the idea that maybe it would be a more relaxed setting if our first meeting would be in the country—at my farm home. When he came to my rural house and stepped in, his first question to me was, 'Mrs. Thatcher, I see the workers are harvesting the fields. Tell me, how in England do you get the food from the farms to the tables of the people? We have real problems here,' he confessed to me."

"When he said that," she continued, locking eyes with Gorbachev, "I was shocked. It was the first time I'd ever heard a Communist world leader admit that their system wasn't really working. I sensed then and there, we can work with this man."

In that simple setting, Margaret Thatcher experienced a new possibility, and history started an amazing shift!

Near the end of the day-long free-for-all discussion in Colorado, Gorbachev made an amazing little speech: "Many factors caused the Cold War to end. But you should know it started before the reform movement began in my country. Years before, I said to President Chernenko, 'Mr. President, we have big problems in our country.'

"'Oh!? What's wrong?' he asked.

"'The system as is isn't working,' I said. Then I explained, 'People aren't as productive as they could and should be.'

"'How long has it been going on like this?' Chernenko asked me.

"And I answered, 'Since 1918, sir—since the Revolution!'"

Before the world leaders departed, Mikhail Gorbachev told me privately that the Communist system in the Soviet Union had failed.

"What you created," I said to him, "was the most powerful national paternalistic system ever devised and imposed on people."

His stunned eyes connected with mine as he sadly nodded his agreement.

J. F. Kennedy hit hard the negative force of paternalism when he said, "Ask not what your country can do for you; ask what you can do for your country."

Well-meaning politics, well-meaning parents, and well-meaning religion—all these can promote paternalism.

Rule 3

BREAK FREE FROM PREJUDICE

What holds us back? Sometimes it's prejudice. We live in a world filled with racial, religious, political, economic, and academic prejudices, and they poison the human potential!

Prejudice tends to intimidate and manipulate us. Prejudice closes doors that should be open to us. Prejudice withholds invitations to join the world's circles of achievers. But the really damnable injury that prejudice inflicts on its innocent victims is what the victims often impose on themselves: the negative reactions of rage, anger, feelings of inferiority, depression, and self-flagellation. Intimidated! Manipulated! Prejudice wins again. The alternative? Get motivated!

My friend Dr. Lonnie Bristow was born in Harlem, where many of the black children grew up infected with an impossibility complex spread by an insidious racism. Then how did Lonnie become a possibility thinker? When he reached the age of twelve, his parents gave him the responsibility to walk each evening to the hospital where his mother was a nurse. He had to wait outside the emergency room door for his mother to finish her shift at 11:00 P.M. His job was to walk her safely home to their apartment. Lonnie's father was a Baptist minister. He taught his children that the Bible is God's Word and that it teaches that all humans are equally loved by the Lord. "God believes in you," he said to Lonnie. "You can do anything, be anyone, and go anywhere you want."

Dr. Bristow shared some of his thinking with me: "I had an opportunity to sometimes see my mother and the other nurses and doctors working in the emergency room. And to me it was inspirational. I could see that it wasn't only multiracial but also multicultural. Those men and women, to me, seemed to have healing qualities in both their hands and more importantly in their hearts. I grew up thinking of them as heroes and wanting to be just like them. Years later, when I was able to go to medical school and become a doctor, I found that the dream I had then was true. That the ability to make a difference in the life of another human being is an enormous thrill—one that I've been able to enjoy now for almost forty years, and it never loses the excitement."

I write these pages only four days after that young boy, now a medical doctor and president of the American Society of Internal Medicine, was my guest on *The Hour of Power.* In 1977 he was elected to membership in the Institute of Medicine of the National Academy of Sciences. He holds three honorary doctor of science degrees. He's currently on the staff of Brookside Hospital, San Pablo, California, and has been on the board of trustees of the American Medical Association since 1985.

I asked Dr. Bristow, "Didn't you ever have impossibility thoughts going through your mind, saying, 'Well, I guess I can't become a doctor; it's going to be too much money,' and so on?"

Dr. Bristow replied, "Well, of course everyone has thoughts like that. I learned early in my life when I was playing football that it's very dangerous to have negative thoughts. I was playing a game once, a very important game. I was running across the goal line as a pass was coming to me. I was perfectly in the clear and the thought entered my mind, wouldn't I look foolish if I dropped this ball. Unfortunately, I did. That was when I learned to never allow negative thoughts to come into my mind. Think positive. See yourself accomplishing that which you want to do. It's worked very well for me ever since. I give to many youngsters in my practice what I call 'Dr. Lonnie's five-point prescription for success in life.'

"First, get serious. Second, stay in school. Three, set a goal. Four, work hard for it. And five, respect yourself in mind, body, and spirit. And always remember that the world really doesn't care how difficult it is for you to get from point A to point B. All the world wants to know is whether you've reached point B and are qualified to provide the service that you want to offer. So don't complain about the difficulty; get on with it. And the last thing I tell my kids in practice is to remember this: Quitters never win and winners never quit!

"As a Christian, I learned certain principles that are most important to me. It's more important to live my beliefs than it is to try to convince others of them by my words. Deeds are what count."

"I'm too old . . . "

There's enough youth-fueled prejudice against age to intimidate many mature adults with an impossibility-thinking complex. "You're past fifty! You're too old to start a new career," some interfering young person says. Soon you repeat the same prejudice to yourself, beginning to believe it. And yet someone else of the same age suddenly changes tracks and gets off the wide road of crowded negative thinking onto a fresh-focused, narrow way empowered by an inspiring possibility!

Enter Cory SerVaas. Now Cory was always a possibility thinker. As a young college graduate she went to New York to work. A single career girl, Cory took a weekend break in the Caribbean. "No walking in swimsuits through the hotel lobby without a cover-up," a sign read. But Cory didn't have the spare dollars to buy a skirt to cover her swimsuit as she walked from her room to the pool. "Think possibilities," she told herself. And that's exactly what she did. She took a wire coat hanger from her hotel closet, broke it, and bent it into a "belt" to which she attached a towel, and with this she walked through the crowded lobby. It worked wonderfully. "I could have a plastic belt made, and something like this could make a simple, inexpensive cover," she thought. Back in New York she made a few calls, and had a few of her hoop skirts made. They sold out quickly. Within a year her simple "invention" was carried by a national chain store, and, as a result, she became financially independent in her early twenties.

Cory married and settled down to live as a wife and mother. She gave birth to five children, enough to keep her busy for the next quarter-century. Where did the years go? When the children were grown, she wondered what she should do. She asked herself this question: "What would you do if you knew you couldn't fail?" Why, she'd become a doctor to give free medical advice to people who needed help. And that's just what Cory did! Her powerful possibility-pregnant dream took hold. She went for it and earned her medical degree when she was past fifty years of age.

Now what would she do? She had another dream: to become a newspaper columnist and share her medical know-how with her readers for free. When she was rejected as a "writer," she bought the bankrupt *Saturday Evening Post* so that she could give herself a journalism job!

Then she dreamed yet another dream.

The secret of success is to find a need and fill it. "I can do research too," she thought. When she heard of a place in Africa where there was little or no colon cancer, she connected with researchers and was a pioneer in publishing their findings throughout America. With her message that low-fat, high-roughage diets seemed to be the secret of the Africans' good health, she helped launch the trend toward a bran-rich diet. Not intimidated, not manipulated, but motivated! That's Cory SerVass!

What holds us back? Provincialism? Paternalism? Prejudice? Or could it be power circles?

Rule 4

BREAK FREE FROM
OPPRESSIVE POWER CIRCLES

Power circles are systemic in society. You're "out" if "in" people give you the impression that you can't make it unless you're invited into their power circle. And the "in" people don't simply open the closely guarded doors to their private club to anyone and everyone. Their inner circle is open only to those who have power to match theirs. "Power-circling," I call it.

It's understandable. The intellectual elite are stimulated and challenged only by bright minds. The really great golfers don't care to play with losers or stumbling, fumbling beginners. The power players are neither challenged—nor helped—except by those who bring something new, or better, to the table.

It's been fascinating to me to see this power play at work at every economic level. The poor have their power circle. The affluent have theirs. And the wealthy have theirs too. So do the super-rich. And the players in each circle aren't attracted to play or work at the table with those in a lower league. Every profession, trade, and career has "ladders" that rise through "leagues"—the equivalent of going from the sandlot, to college play, to professional farm teams, and finally up to the major leagues. I've been and am a pastor to persons at all economic levels. I've observed that the rich choose to run with those in their own league. And the very wealthy aren't attracted to the rich who run in a smaller league—but they're attracted to and challenged by the very rich in the higher circles. They belong to different and exclusive clubs.

Big players simply aren't challenged by the smaller players. People figure, "Let the rookies rise and earn their place, and then they can and will break through into the bigger game." It happens all the time.

Yes, every power circle rides on its own pride and prejudices. Right or wrong. The real question is How do we handle this if we're out and want to be in? The "power prejudice" isn't the problem that can defeat us. The only really damaging decision is our own reaction to that prejudice. React positively—be challenged by it—and it will turn into a powerful motivator to drive you to success! React negatively to the prejudice, and you'll annihilate your own dreams!

Weigh the possibilities in and around the power circle.

Power circles are all around us. They're racial, they're religious, they're political, they're economic, they're academic, they're social, they're scientific, they're cultural, they're corporate, and more. These power circles are good at their best and bad at their worst.

There are masculine power circles and feminine power circles. Chauvinism? Of course. Most power circles are chauvinistic.

Skill isn't—and shouldn't be—shared at the controls with the unskilled. Imagine that we're passengers on a jetliner. We're all in danger if the power and control aren't in the best-trained and most skilled hands. Excellence mustn't share its position, its power, and its control with mediocrity. Professionals mustn't share final control with amateurs. Everyone can be hurt if that dictum is violated. Power circles. That's what life's about. We're in—or we're out.

Each power circle consists of an invisible collection of ever-enlarging circles, like those on an archer's target. At the center is the bull's-eye—call it the power core. The bull's-eye is never a small group; it's always a single person. The power always starts and stops with one person. Around that solitary power there's a very small circle. These are the people who surround the controlling power heart. This first circle around the bull's-eye is the power center. Surrounding this elite circle is the next larger circle, which picks up energy from the power center and carries out the mission. People in this echelon surround the power center, executing the power center's ideas. They report back to the power center on what works and what doesn't work. Another larger circle surrounds this circle. People here experience diminishing power to plan, to dream, and to execute the central mission. There may be yet another outside, larger circle that serves as the boundary of the enterprise, be it an institution, a corporation, or a movement.

If you're beyond even this outside circle, you may be on the edge looking in—but you're still out. How do you get in? The controllers are careful of whom they invite, both to join from outside and to move from a larger circle into a smaller one. Credentials, accountability, and discipline become more severe as outsiders make their way toward the power center.

An atmosphere that vibrates with professional prejudice can intimidate those who wish they were in and not out. How do you break through? These simple guidelines offer some insight:

1. **Never let power prejudice be seen as a negative, oppressive force to keep you out**. Believe the best—not the worst. Believe that all exclusive power circles must be dedicated and disciplined to maintain or achieve excellence, and to immunize the power center from becoming infected and inflicted with a subtle mediocrity. Believe that somehow, someway, sometime you can break through this prejudging atmosphere and be invited in. Catch a vision of how packed with possibilities your life would be if you were part of the power circle you're eyeing.

2. **Believe it's possible to break through and break in.** Everyone in every power circle needs to be replaced sometime by someone. Weigh the possibilities carefully. Remember that good luck is preparation that runs into opportunity.

3. **Weigh the possibilities on your personal -mission scale, and then learn the rules.** Is this the place where you can best fulfill your mission

in life? If not, forget it. If so—if this is the place where your life's purpose could and would be fulfilled—find out what the requirements for admission really are. What are the rules to be followed to enter and rise in this circle?

4. **Now weigh the possibilities on your moral scale.** If you pursue this power circle, what moral and ethical demands will it impose upon you? Weigh the possibilities wisely. What will the passionate pursuit of enticing and exciting possibilities do to you?

It's important to remember that possibilities never leave you where they found you. Every new possibility pursued with passion changes the hunter somehow, someway. Will the hunt force discipline upon you to make you, slowly but surely, a better man or woman? A better husband or wife? A better father or mother? A better neighbor or friend?

Weigh the possibilities carefully and prayerfully. Is the signal that attracted you growing weaker or even breaking up altogether? Then shift your gears to neutral. If the game calls for something illegal, immoral, or unethical, back up and get out. On the other hand, as you weigh the enticing possibilities on your moral scale, is the signal to strive and succeed becoming stronger, steadier, and more inspirationally alluring?

5. **Shift into a forward gear.** Do you sense an agonizing contradiction in your heart and soul? Do you feel a powerful attraction to go for it—but at the same time a gnawing anxiety, even a fear of failure? Don't turn the switch off! Try shifting to a low forward gear.

You've weighed the possibilities. The scales say go. So put your safety belt on and firmly grip the steering wheel. You're the driver. You're no longer an outside observer. Your future is in your hands. Start your engine. Go for the power circle!

6. **Keep open one nonnegotiable option— to create your own power circle.** What if you stay with the rules, earn your credentials, and play the politics honestly and honorably, but the bureaucrats in the power circle still won't accept you into the inner circles, where you're qualified to sit and where your potential can be released?

What if you're still out and not in? Then what? Then start your own power circle and become a creative competitor. You can posture and position yourself to be the heart of a new power circle that's more interested in your dream than any other power circle can or will be. At the heart of a new circle, you'll be free to try innovations that the secure and success-

Keep
. . . .
your eye
. . . .
on your
. . . .
heroes,
. . . .
not on
. . . .
your
. . . .
zeroes.
. . . .

ful older power circles shy away from.

As a young professional minister I was very uneasy about power circles in religious establishments. I knew I wasn't lazy. Quite the contrary: I was ambitious. That scared me. I decided never to aim to become an inside member of any power circle. I'd simply start my own church and make it into the most powerful and positive ministry that I could, with the help of God.

Now let me invite you to become an inside member of a fantastic power circle. "If it's going to be, it's up to me!" is the key you need to open the door to a power circle called the Possibility Thinkers' Club. You're invited to come into this power circle now. It's free. You'll move from out to in right here! Right now! And from here you'll go on to greater power circles!

Rule 5

BREAK FREE FROM POVERTY

Yes, poverty holds people back from seeing and seizing their potential. Is this what's holding you back? One of the most insightful perspectives I ever heard on poverty was offered by the esteemed U.S. Congressman Charles Rangel on *The Larry King Show*. Rangel was born into poverty in Harlem and went from the periphery to the center of America's foremost power circles.

"Poverty," he said, "is no big deal. Almost all of the immigrants that came to this country were poor. What is a big deal is that a person has to have dreams and believe he can make it!" Then wisely he added, "And that's where education comes in."

In the full life I've lived, I've learned and now declare that no person, no institution, and no business ever has a money problem. It's never a money problem. It's always an idea problem. Money? There's so much of it! And money is always on the move—looking for new persons with bright ideas!

The truly crippling poverty that destroys persons is emotional poverty, and possibility thinking can attack that sort of poverty powerfully.

<u>Rule 6</u>

BREAK FREE FROM PROSPERITY

Prosperity: Could that be the enemy blinding you to bigger, better, more beautiful possibilities?

The greatest temptation to lure us from achieving our true potential comes for many possibility thinkers not at the dreaming or striving stages but at the arriving stage! In fact, that's the stage at which the greatest possibilities are dropped.

"I've worked so hard to get it. I'm going to retire and enjoy it." Or "I earned it. I deserve it!"

Careful! Success mustn't be trapped by stagnation. Success must move on to significance. And significance must move on to satisfaction. And satisfaction awaits the socially and spiritually sensitive achiever who turns his or her back on the alluring call to self-indulgence.

Prosperity can put the brakes on a movement that's dynamically exploring the possibilities that still slumber and sleep!

Success can so easily tempt the prosperous to a retirement that can best be described as unrestricted self-indulgence. Have fun. Relax. Play golf. Garden. Travel. Is this the end goal of prosperity? For many, apparently, the answer is yes.

What's beyond success? Stagnation? Self-indulgence? Or continuing significance? Maximum satisfaction comes only as new possibilities are turned into new goals to reenergize the human spirit.

Prosperity comes with a siren call to lie back and enjoy life. Its tempting voice can manipulate so deceptively. "You've got more than you could ever enjoy. Retire! You don't need or want more—unless you're greedy!"

Yes, prosperity can do you in. Real selfish satisfaction has a short span.

Success must move on to significance or it corrodes. Which explains why the greatest possibility thinkers keep thinking bigger.

Are the super-rich driven by greed? Yes, some are, even though they couldn't possibly enjoy any more money. Why aren't they content with all they have? Why do multi-millionaires allow themselves to become billionaires? Greed? Arrogance? Be slow to fall for this negative assumption. For many successful persons, the motive is very honorable. Many extremely rich people I've known are driven by the passion to "do more real good for more people." They've become philanthropists because they know that many great causes depend on private funding. And they're familiar with the saying, "Money follows money." The more they give, the more they feel the call to do more. Many of my successful Christian friends are driven by need—the need to help others—more than greed.

They've discovered that success is power. The power to fight poverty positively, for example, and to make the world a better and more beautiful place.

Success carries with it a heavy responsibility. Call it stewardship, if you will. Achievers have learned that it's impossible to succeed without helping people who need help. Success is found in this simple principle that they've learned: "Find a need and fill it."

In building their professional career or their business, achievers need good people. As a consequence, many of the really unselfish superprosperous people strive to create more job opportunities, to make and market goods and services that people need and want.

From their platform of prosperity and their position of power, they can leverage their resources to grow larger and go further. And who are the real beneficiaries? The super-rich—for they stay alive! They must be expandable—or they'll be expendable! The deepest need is the need to be needed! They see a crowd of persons who desire a chance to make their dreams come true too. The "wanna-be's" need help if they're ever going to become "gonna-be's." So the supersuccessful persons break free from their prosperity by helping people rise from poverty to affluence, from affluence to prosperity, and from prosperity to philanthropy!

What's blocking

your advancement?

Provincialism?

Paternalism?

Prejudice?

Power circles?

Poverty? Prosperity?

or simply Problems?

Rule 7

BREAK FREE FROM PROBLEMS

Do problems in general numb you? Then get smart and find out what the real problems are that block you.

Good news! There's a solution to your biggest problem!

For the only real problem that can torpedo and sink you is one person.

- That person is someone you must talk to.
- That person is someone you can talk to.
- That person is someone who will listen to you.
- That person is someone you can change from a negative person into a positive person.
- That person can be converted from a "put-you-down enemy" into a "build-you-up friend."
- That person is someone you can change from an obstructionist into a doer who can remove obstacles, open doors, and make contacts with smarter, more skillful, wealthier people.
- That person is someone who can help you to discover hidden talent slumbering within you.

- That person is someone who can motivate, encourage, inspire, enthuse, and energize you to get and stay on the narrow way to real success!
- That person—your only real problem— is someone who can and must be won over to become your best friend.

That person who is your only serious problem and will become your best booster is you! So you can and must stop being your biggest problem and become your biggest asset instead.

You must—absolutely must—believe in yourself!

It's up to you to make your dream come true!

"If it's going to be, it's up to me!"

Yes, your only real problem is the person who could cause you to take your eyes off your goal. The only serious problem you have is the one person who has the power to pull you away from the pursuit of your dream. And there's only one person who has the authority to order you to give up on your possibilities. That person is you!

Other frustrations, factors, fears, forces, and faces can block you temporarily. Others can advise, recommend, encourage, or discourage you, but the final decision can be made only by the person who sits behind your desk.

You were born to inherit the job that makes you the president and chief executive officer charged with the responsibility of managing your inner potential. Destiny has appointed you to sit in the chair as the ultimate controller of your future.

You'll face difficulties that may or may not be of your making. You must expect an assortment of adversities that won't be your fault; but in every case you—and no one else but you—must assume the personal responsibility to select the smartest response and reaction to these challenges.

The most important documents that shape your future will require and accept only one signature. That signature is yours and yours alone. No proxy is acceptable. The certificate is titled: "My Dream! My Goal. And I promise God—I will pursue the dream He's giving me!" Sign it, and you'll have solved your biggest problem.

Beginning is half done. Start by dealing with your first and foremost problem, the problem that you alone can and must solve. That problem is a person—called you! Yes, you are your biggest problem if and when you take your eyes off of your God-given goal and close your eyes and ears to God's call to go for it!

Now you see it: the only problem that can hold you back isn't provincialism, paternalism, prejudice, power circles, poverty, or prosperity. It's the person you see in the mirror every morning! It's the person whose head you put to the pillow every night!

And you can solve this problem when you make a decision to become and remain a possibility thinker!

So you don't have a problem after all! You've only got a decision to make.

Yes, all problems are really illusions. In reality, every problem is only a decision waiting to be made. And you're in control. You alone have the freedom, the authority, and the power to make that one decision that will solve your biggest problem! You can simply decide to become a success!

Weigh the possibility carefully and prayerfully.

What would be a fantastic achievement, a miraculous and meaningful success, if you could pull it off? Would the dividends paid by this investment of your resources be really wonderful? For you yourself? Your family? Your community? Your country? Would the returns make a beautiful, honorable difference in the lives you value most? Weighed on the scale of the most respected human values, how does the possibility rate? Go for it? Congratulations! You're already a winner in the first phase of possibility thinking!

Will your possibility free you? Yes! You're now free from inertia! Free from indecision! Free from the imprisoning fear of failure! These invisible bars that have kept your potential locked up are now open. The lack of self-confidence that's barred you is now bending under the positive pressure of the words you affirmed to yourself and to the world: "I think I can! I believe that it's possible. I'm going to try!"

—⚶—

I'm not free till I believe in me.

—⚶—

Be sure of this: God has designed human beings to be the one and only creature that differs from all animals by having the power to conceive of the possibility of an invisible, creative Higher Power we call God. This eternal and intelligent energy is constantly sending creative ideas into human minds. And if God

I'm
going
to
decide
to
succeed.

can inspire me to believe it, He can help me to achieve it.

"What's the eternal, affectionate, redemptive Higher Power called God trying to tell me today?" I ask. And God answers, "Believe in me! Believe in the positive ideas I'm sending you! Believe in yourself—I do!" That's the message God is trying to get into all of our human heads and hearts today!

Change or chains: it's every person's choice, here and now. Every person has been created to be creative. Every person has the power to imagine what he or she could do and be. And every person is exposed to great possibilities.

Herman Cain is a wonderful success story that illustrates this point. He's an African-American who was raised in a one-room apartment.

"Someday I'm going to buy and own a whole house," his father promised his wife and two little boys. So he held down three jobs: chauffeur, janitor, and butcher.

He succeeded, one dollar at a time! What he gave to his little boy was a powerful message: "I'm free—if I'll believe in me." So Herman set his goals high too. He'd go to college. He'd become so well educated that good companies would want to hire him. Self-confidence—he got it. He went on to earn his master's degree and became vice-president of the Pillsbury Company. When they were having problems with one of their subsidiaries, Godfather's Pizza, Herman was offered the chance to buy it— cheap! He made the move, turning it into one of America's corporate success stories. He's one of my heroes! I was honored to nominate him for membership in the Horatio Alger Association. Only ten persons are elected to that group each year, and he was one of them in 1996. When the honorees were asked to share the decision that most impacted their achievement, he responded, "For me that's easy to answer. It was when I decided to succeed."

Well, that's where you are—here and now! Make that decision, and you're on your way. Just decide, "I'm going to succeed," and you may become the owner of your own company: My Dream, Inc. Get set now to assume the management of a fantastic new career, profession, or business!

Is there an obstacle to your advancement I haven't touched? Then you must name it, claim your right, and unlock your possibility! That's your responsibility.

Possibilities have been weighed. Now priorities must be swayed.

II

PRIORITIES
MUST BE SWAYED

———∽∽∽———

"This possibility thinking is going to kill us all off!" I was shocked to hear these words! For a brief moment my closest associate, Wilbert Eichenberger, was overwhelmed with more exciting opportunities than his overloaded imagination was equipped to manage.

Mental overload. Is that what dynamic, creative possibility thinkers have to deal with? Quite possibly. Which simply means that we must be smart at swaying priorities.

You don't have room for everyone in your car? Then who stays home? And who goes?

You don't have room in your suitcase? Then what gets left behind? What's the first thing you must pack?

You blew a fuse? Electrical overload. With extra appliances needed to prepare food for the party, what plugs get pulled out? What can wait?

Is your mind like a clothes closet? Perhaps you don't realize how many ideas have been allowed to accumulate in your consciousness, rather like garments collected through the years and allowed to hang disorganized in a jammed closet. Now—out of the blue—come fresh possibilities that certainly deserve to be welcomed into the private room of your consciousness. And there's no room for them? You have no space left? You're mentally overloaded? What do you do?

It's time to reorganize the overcrowded storeroom of ideas in your mind, to clear out and clean off the mental shelves just as you get rid of clutter in the closet. Many old ideas are hang-ups. Throw them out. Sort through your mental wardrobe. What in the world is all this? How can there be so much stuff in this one mind? Where did it all come from, and when? What a collection of mental memorabilia! There's so much that you'll never need again.

You're on the move to a new you, on the way to a new world. What do you keep? What do you throw away or give away to make room for exciting new possibilities? It's time to choose your failures carefully. I've chosen to fail at golf, for example. I gave it up, period! I've chosen instead to use my time to succeed with a higher priority and build a church that I believe can make a difference in the world.

From possibilitizing to prioritizing. That's where you are. Possibilities have been weighed; now priorities must be swayed.

—∿—

If it's going to be, it's up to me!

—∿—

Only you can choose what load your mind can carry. You and you alone can unlock that private door in your mind to the storeroom loaded with possibilities. You and you alone know what you've collected there. Trash or treasure? Classic and timeless or worn out and outdated? You and you alone can bring about the long-overdue mental reorganization in that storeroom.

Prioritize. What does this really mean? It means saying goodbye to ideas that have lost their value because of competition from new possibilities that have come to you. It means saying hello to new ideas whose time has come! It means saying wait to ideas that have been upstaged by a surprising new opportunity of greater value—an opportunity that cannot and will not wait.

So smart, successful possibility thinkers are tough on themselves in shifting and swaying priorities. Perhaps you've heard this saying: "Tough times never last—but tough people do."

Unlock your private door. Here, in the sheltered safety of secure solitude, strip off the embarrassing, ill-fitting assortment of ideas you bought and closeted—ideas that now hang in your mind like old garments that no longer deserve the place you gave to them.

Some are ideas that were given to you and that you accepted unhesitatingly, too intimidated to reject or discard them. Others are ideas that you believed in passionately for a time but then lost interest.

Now's the time to disrobe your imagination. Clear out all those old mental hang-ups. Clear out dated possibilities that you've allowed to oppressively overcrowd your imagination over the years. Strip away any extraneous ideas—even those that are good (and some of them are)—to make room for better and more beautiful dreams. Clear out the closet! You're free! Free to peruse and pursue fresh new dreams.

Today you're becoming a new you, and you've been given the best gift ever! You're invited to select a completely new wardrobe of dynamic ideas, positive possibilities. You can choose the style and size!

Yes, bravely do what you should have done long ago: reorganize your mental closet. Wisely save the precious ideas that you should never discard. But clear out all the junk that still hangs in the crammed shadows of your soul—all those hang-ups, judgments, oppressive low-self-esteem complexes, and self-deprecating attitudes. Yes—out! Away! Gone!

A whole new mental wardrobe is needed.

———— ∿ ————

Dare to be a new you!

———— ∿ ————

Anything is possible! Now that you've cleaned out your closet, go on a mental shopping spree in places you've never dared to go before! Find out what's out there waiting for a new you.

You ask, "Am I really totally free to dream any dream?" Yes. You're free to become a new you!

"Are there no boundaries to what I'm free to imagine?" None. No boundaries, no limits, except for those implicit in:

Civil law
Moral law
Ethical principles
Religious scruples
Personal commitments to family and
top-priority relationships

"Does that mean that I have complete liberty
to take on any new dream?" you ask.

Yes, if in Chapter 1 you weighed new possibilities carefully and prayerfully on the morality
and personal-mission scales.

Now that you're ready to move on, priorities
must be checked, double-checked, and re-
checked. For some of the biggest, brightest,
best, and most beautiful dreams your imagination encounters will be, for the moment, imprac-
tical, impossible, or improbable. Let's be honest:
"Great idea, but I'm already overcommitted,"
you say, and you're correct.

Now that we agree, let's get practical. Let's
not disregard a fresh, inspiring new idea simply
because it's impossible or overwhelming. Impossibilities become possibilities when someone—perhaps you?—deliberately challenges
his or her priorities. New dreams and inspiring
new goals often demand the updating and revision of prelaid plans and priorities.

I'll have to cancel my plans.
I'll have to postpone my intentions.
I'll have to reorganize.
I'll have to refinance.
I'll have to go back to the drawing board.
I'll have to take a fresh look at my calendar.
I'll have to challenge my assumptions.
I'll have to talk to smarter people.

When possibility thinkers are surprised by a spontaneous and unexpected opportunity, they don't irresponsibly seize it. Nor do they (with equal irresponsibility) allow the suggestion to be dismissed, offhand and outright, with a careless, cavalier negative response. Instead, they treat the fresh possibility with reverent respect: "I'll take a new look at my schedule. Perhaps I'll need to realign my priorities."

Of course, there will be risks. Every decision commands a price—known or unknown. But you can't escape all risks by avoiding all risks. Remember, before you turn your back on the new possibility, that you risk losing what you might have won. The saddest words of tongue or pen are these—It might have been.

The Quakers were taught to pray each night before they went to sleep. They were also taught to pray on awakening each morning,

If you get where you're going, where will you be?

seeking divine wisdom by drawing up a fresh list of what they could do that day. The new day might be a virtual repeat of the day before, but not necessarily! The morning news comes on. An unexpected telephone call interrupts the day's plans. Or a conversation you had with someone changes priorities with a new idea!

Providence often challenges our careful planning with an uninvited and unexpected fresh possibility! So make out your new priority list every morning. You'll be surprised at how frequently your priorities can and should be urgently, wisely, even compassionately revised.

I'm living what I've just written. Well over a year ago I accepted an invitation to deliver a speech, only to find, as the date drew near, that the host had become involved in a headline-making controversy. I received a telephone call one day informing me that I too was front-page news. A newspaper story mentioned that my controversial host was bringing Schuller out to speak. The implication? That I was taking his side. Well, I had a host of friends on both sides of the issue. The host and I talked, we negotiated, and, under the circumstances, we agreed together that I shouldn't go. A new story appeared: "Given the politicking and the polarization of the controversial issue, the invitation to Schuller to speak has been withdrawn." Everyone agreed that it was the right decision.

Now what would I do with the sudden, unexpected opening of three days on my calendar? Would I take a three-day holiday? Would I catch up on my office work? Would I make necessary pastoral calls? Would I schedule meetings focusing on my recently announced ten-year goals? Would I catch up on all of the reading I had no time to do otherwise? Or would I slip out of the area, seclude myself in a secret place, and write the book that had to be finished and delivered to the publisher in three months? My decision? To take advantage of the free time to work on the book; that was my first priority.

For me this was a challenging decision. As I booked the plane flight to a place of solitude, I wondered whether I was making the right decision. I now know that I was. But juggling plans, appraising options, evaluating needs, and then ranking priorities isn't easy!

PRINCIPLES FOR PRIORITIZING

Any task is easier if you have the proper tools. While needle-nose pliers won't help you rank your priorities, I can offer seven solid principles of prioritizing that will. Let's take a look.

Principle 1

WRITE YOUR PRIORITIES IN PENCIL, NOT INK

There are priorities that are poured in concrete, of course. My God and my family come first for me, as for all Christians. But all the possibilities from vocation to vacation must be subject to the winds of change that God, society, business, and science may unpredictably blow your way.

The greatest danger a good idea faces is that you'll succumb to the temptation to discard a better opportunity that unexpectedly comes along to compete with the good idea that's in the works—in other words, that you'll carry your idea through when it should have been reprioritized.

"Bob, your dad is dying," my sister said over the phone. "Come home! He wants to see and touch you before he goes." My priorities were swayed; I changed my plans.

Principle 2

CHALLENGE ALL NEGATIVE ASSUMPTIONS

Challenge your assumptions. Manage your assumptions, or they'll manipulate you as you decide on your priorities.

The traffic is stopped on the inside lane,

your lane. Cars are bumper to bumper, and nothing is moving. Several cars, a van, and a small truck are just ahead of you. Do you wait patiently? Blindly? Or do you cut into the outside lane, which is slowly moving?

Your decision—more likely than not—will be based on assumptions.

Relax. Stay where you are. The traffic ahead of you will soon move, and you'll be on your way. You'll get ahead best if you go with the flow. Progress may be slow, but it will happen. Those are assumptions. They may be right; they may be wrong.

Cut out! Switch to the lane that's moving. Never surrender control to something ahead of you that's not moving, that's not going somewhere. Another set of assumptions.

You assume that the plane you're ticketed on will take off on time as you head for an important sales meeting. You have no backup plan. "Flight Canceled" you read when you reach your gate. Shocked, you go to the telephone and make the call: "Sorry. I won't be able to make the appointment." An unchallenged assumption is in control again. Probably you could have flown to a nearby town and rented a car. You could even have chartered a plane! Too expensive? Another assumption.

Perhaps not! It probably would have been possible to reach your destination as scheduled in a private plane—and you might have signed and closed the deal. The added expense might have been worth it!

Let's consider another scenario. You arrive at your hotel. You're in a hurry to reach the second floor. There are three elevators in the ground-floor lobby. You check their indicator lights: one elevator seems to be on the sixth floor, another on the third, and another on the fifth. You watch their movements as if the elevators were horses on a racetrack, and you bet on which one will be the first to come down to your level. Then you notice that next to the elevator is an exit marked Stairs. You're in great shape. Should you wait for the first elevator or run up one flight? Whichever decision you make, it will be based on assumptions.

Take the steps? No assuming there, right? Wrong. You're assuming that there will be a door from the stairwell to the next level. (After all, fire code would require that—right?) You run up. There's a door all right, but it's been locked by the security guard to foot traffic from the stairwell. It's an exit door only! Wrong again. You walk down and wait for the next elevator.

This lesson was clearly brought home to me at a hospital one day. I was interviewing Dr. Michael DeBakey in his office. "How many living human hearts have your hands touched?" I asked.

"Over fifty thousand," he answered.

"How can that be?" I challenged.

"Well, I've been at it for over forty years," he said, his eyes twinkling with pride, "and I do as many as nine surgeries a day! Do you want to see how we do it? Follow me." He walked out of his office, and in a few fast steps he was at the elevators. His eyes swiftly read the score: both elevators were in use. "We'll run up; it's only one flight," he said.

"No patience," I thought to myself.

"I have a rule here," he explained as we walked up the steps. "If I ever catch anyone waiting for the elevator to go up only one flight, that person is fired!" His strong tone of voice indicated to me that he was serious. "You see, Dr. Schuller, you never know if or when the elevator will come. You can't assume it's in service just because you see the lights on. And you can't assume it'll be here fast. We're in the life-and-death business here. You can't take a chance assuming that the elevator will be here soon. My order is strictly and sternly enforced! I'll fire anyone waiting for an elevator to go only one flight up or down."

Priorities? Yes, we're all managed and manipulated by assumptions. Challenge every negative assumption that would block you from upgrading your priorities.

Principle 3
CHECK YOUR MISSION STATEMENT

Just imagine: you're free! Free to privately, personally—yes, passionately—dream your dream.

There are no restrictions, no rules, no regulations to restrain your wild and wonderful flights of fantasy. None save for the appropriate limits you've wisely imposed upon yourself!

No boundaries to fashion or fence your fantasies. Right? Correct!

Which means you must have a concrete core of moral values or you'll be on the broad road that leads to folly and failure. So draft a mission statement and let this be before you each step of the way as you prioritize.

When corporate consultants meet with top corporate officers, they begin by saying, "You must write a mission statement. If your primary mission is to make money, that's okay," they advise, "but if that's the case, say it. That will help you battle the temptation to make decisions that would give a powerful boost to your ego but seriously threaten your company's profitability."

Likewise, they may advise, "If your primary mission is to change society and the world into a more beautiful, healthier human community—even if it puts you in a nonprofit position—that's okay. But declare it! And prepare to succeed by solving the negative cash-flow challenges."

No person, institution, family, or business is qualified to manage until a mission statement is carefully and prayerfully written. Nouns, verbs, adjectives, and adverbs will combine to define your purpose for existing. The mission statement will clarify and verify your moral, spiritual, and ethical values. Until that's done, you'll be ill-prepared to make decisions that make demands on your limited resources of time, money, energy, emotions, organization, strength, relationships, and human health and welfare.

Whatever you do, whoever you are, wherever you hope to go, whatever your mission statement is, it must make room for someone or something beyond yourself.

Of course, ego needs are terribly important. Don't ignore them. You must be proud of who you are, what you've accomplished, and what you hope to do. Yes, do prioritize to plan for achievement that holds the promise of bringing honor and respect to your profession and to your personal reputation. But ego needs give way to a higher priority: helping people with their hopes and their hurts.

The medical doctor finds his greatest reward in seeing wellness come to a person he's helped and healed.

The pastor of a large church finds his greatest satisfaction when he cries alone with a single hurting parishioner.

The professional athletic superstar finds his greatest fulfillment when he teaches kids the tricks of his trade.

The millionaire enjoys his greatest success when he learns that generous giving is real living.

Your mission statement will do more than anything or anyone else to help you rank and rate the opportunities and prioritize your possibilities.

I've often lectured on this all-important lesson: "Faith + Focus + Follow-through = Success." Remember this formula in setting your priorities. A strong mission statement, more than anything else, will protect you from tempting diversions and distractions—alternatives that would allow you to deviate from your primary responsibility and drain crucial resources from your primary priority.

Principle 4

DETECT, DISCOVER, AND TAKE DIRECTION FROM YOUR UNIQUENESS

No two persons are alike. Know yourself. What makes you unique? Are you a mother? No one else can fill that role for your family the way you can. A founder? No one else will see the roots of the business as you do.

"How in the world do you do such a great job running what's become a huge and successful company?" I asked one corporate chief.

He thought for a moment. "I've learned how to set priorities for my time and energy," he answered. "I never do anything if I can find someone else who can do it as well as or better than I can. That leaves me with nothing to do except what I and only I can do."

That advice helped me to set my priorities on how to use those unexpected free days on my calendar. I—and only I—can write my book. No other living human has within his head, heart, soul, experience, and memory system the consciousness that can exactly duplicate the person I am. Prioritize your tasks and goals so that you do what only you can and should do.

Principle 5

CALCULATE THE LIFE SPAN OF THE POSSIBILITIES THAT COMPETE FOR YOUR ATTENTION

By ranking your overloaded possibilities according to their life span, you give top priority to the option with the narrowest window of opportunity. Can this project wait? How long? The offer expires—when? If I wait, will it be cheaper? More costly? Will there be more competition? Must I move fast if I want to be in a position of power?

Check the time limit of all priorities before you rank them. Ask yourself questions such as these:

How long will this opportunity be here for me to grasp?

How fast must I move?

Can I buy time in some way?

If I pass on the opportunity now, will I get another chance?

Will anything be cheaper or better if I wait? If so, how long should I wait?

If I pass on this opportunity, will it seriously negatively impact my mission? Will it close important doors?

Is this opportunity vital to my immediate or long-range goals?

If I take this opportunity, who or what will have to go on a waiting list for my attention? Can that person or project wait? If not, can I find someone else to fill in for me?

Is there any competition? What else is coming on line? Will increased competition drive the price down? Can I live with that? Will a potential competitor help or hurt me? When will he or she make a move? Should we form a coalition?

If I give this new idea top priority, what are its chances of success? Can I live with failure?

How do I want to be remembered? What kind of reputation do I seek?

Would it be wise to wait? One of America's most popular radio shows in the 1950s was hosted by the late, great choral conductor Fred Waring. Known as *The Fred Waring Hour with the Pennsylvanians,* the show offered beautiful music. Fred Waring's fame was considerable: a major street in Palm Springs, California—near Bob Hope Avenue and Frank Sinatra Avenue—was named after him.

Less well known is Fred Waring's invention, which he wisely chose not to patent. He invented a machine that could mix beverages with ground-up ice cubes and called it a "blender." He told me about his decision not to patent: "Well, there was no established market for it. No one had ever heard of such an apparatus. It would take millions and millions of dollars to buy the advertising needed to enlighten the public with this great new thing I had come up with. So I took it to the big companies. They saw its possibilities and copied my invention. Overnight several large electrical appliance companies began selling this new appliance called the 'blender.' They created the market. Then I simply came in with mine—the original, the one and only Waring Blender."

Principle 6

BE HUMBLE ENOUGH—AND BRAVE ENOUGH—TO DARE TO ASK FOR HELP

Setting priorities? One of my heroes is Stan Hubbard, whose great family brought the daily newspaper, as well as radio and television, to Minneapolis and St. Paul. Let me tell you about something he taught me.

One of my high priorities is raising the funds to keep our nonprofit ministry alive. One year we had a shortfall of three million dollars. What to do? Fold the ministry? Scale back? Or ask for more help? We opted for—no, we're addicted to!—possibility thinking. We decided to seek help.

"Pride goes before destruction" (Proverbs 16:18), the Bible says. How many people fail because they don't see priorities wisely? And how often is a positive idea denied top priority because we don't want to ask for the help we know we need or because we don't want to share the credit?

Dare to ask for help! Smart people who are humble enough to admit that they need help— and are willing to share the power and glory of their success—will find amazing support from wonderful strangers. Here's the exciting promise of the first of the beatitudes of Jesus: "Blessed are the poor in spirit for theirs is the Kingdom of Heaven" (Matthew 5:3).

So I made an appointment to see Stan Hubbard, who's always ready to see me.

"What brings you to town, Bob?" he asked.

I made my presentation and asked him for a million-dollar gift. Hardly were the words out of my mouth when he said, "No. No, I won't help you. I didn't say 'can't,' I said 'won't.' I have a goal to be first in putting direct satellite broadcasting in business. See this dish, only a little over a foot in size? Well, I'll put a broadcast satellite in space and anyone, anywhere in the whole USA, can pick it up with this small aerial! And we'll be sending dozens of channels! Now, you can buy cable, of course—but we'll offer more (and I think better) programming!"

His enthusiasm grew as he described his project. "I'm going to do it! I'm putting all my money in that project—nearly a hundred million dollars already! So that's why my answer is no to you today."

Then he smiled and added, "But I'll make you a promise. It fits with my mission, and it fits with your mission too. When I get that satellite up there, I'll put your show, *The Hour of Power,* on the air on the very first Sunday in the history of DBS television!

"You know I have to charge you now for airing your show here in Minnesota. But I'll make you a promise: I'll put you on my new station for free! And I'll keep you on every week as long as our family owns the station—free! Now I'll call in my sons and we'll all shake hands on this. The Hubbard family keeps its word! Come in, boys! Bob, you know how expensive it is to buy TV air time. The gift we're promising you will add up to a lot more than a million dollars."

How Stan Hubbard pulled it off is truly history! I was delighted to be invited to the launch and then, from a distance, to watch it succeed. One day soon after the launch a phone call came from the office of the DBS television station. "Dr. Schuller," an enthusiastic voice announced, "we're turning the power on next Sunday, and you'll be on it—the first church service in history to be seen via direct satellite broadcasting! We're sending you a dish so that you can enjoy it!" And that's the story behind Stan Hubbard's dynamic business, USSB. A hinge in history. Stan Hubbard saw the possibilities, and he set a schedule that honored his priorities.

Make a list of all of your possibilities. From among those, select your top priorities. Time those priorities. Let those priorities compete with each other to win your attention and your investment.

Don't be intimidated by past decisions. Don't be emotionally manipulated by the projects at the top of your "priority ladder." Let them confront and be challenged by the competition of the new opportunity before you. Force your well-ingrained ideas to be measured against the changes you're looking at!

Principle 7

APPRAISE YOUR POWER BASE

Your strength will determine what possibilities you can and cannot prioritize.

How strong and how solid is your power base? You can't jump from a falling ladder. Floating or swimming is likewise no base for taking a leap; water is no power base for a controlled flying plunge that requires solid footing. A few days ago I tried to step from a boat to the slip where the craft was tied. I didn't notice that the ropes meant to stabilize and secure the boat to the pier weren't pulled tightly. Nor did I notice that a wind had come up, silent and strong. The unanticipated result? The distance from my base to my goal looked to be about thirty inches. Just one easy step and I'd move from the boat to the solid cement pier. With my left foot firmly planted on the rear deck of the boat and my right foot raised in transit, my body shifted weight to make the safe step.

Suddenly a surge of wind moved the rear of the boat at least another foot from the slip, expanding the space between my left foot—still solidly grounded on what was now a shifting power base—and the walkway that my right foot was almost touching (and toward which my in-the-air body was falling). The gap between my two legs was now four feet, not thirty inches. So my right foot missed the solid walkway and I fell! Backed by my full body weight of over two hundred pounds, my unguarded right thigh slammed against the hard side of the pier. My right foot, instead of landing on the dry walkway, was in the water; my left foot hovered just at the surface. I'd missed the leap by twelve inches. My arms and my chest fell hard, fast, flat, and painfully on the concrete pier. My hands grasped for and grabbed a rope, so I was spared from falling completely overboard in water ten feet deep. Wow! How stable is your power base?

In sizing up your priorities, carefully appraise your power base. Then check again, carefully! The power base is probably shifting. Check a third time before you make a move that could throw you dangerously out of control.

Before property is purchased, the lending agency often (and wisely) requires an up-to-date appraisal of the property's value. Not one but three separate appraisals by certified, credentialed appraisal firms are sometimes required. The bank adds up the bottom-line dollar amounts of those appraisals, divides by three, and produces a responsible "average." That number then determines the base for the collateral power of the loan. You can apply that same appraisal process in upgrading or downgrading your power base.

The following seven significant elements should be calculated to appraise your power base:

Concept
Calendar
Character
Connections
Cash
Competition
Check your flexibility

Check each element out. Measure and weigh them. Analyze and understand them. Value the importance of each one as you wisely seek to minimize the risks.

Don't exaggerate either your actual or your potential power base. When you're planning a parachute, it's smarter to underestimate than to exaggerate its lifesaving possibility.

Concept. The idea—the possibility-impregnated concept—is at the heart of every power base. Ideas have value.

Are you a visionary?

I've seen creative people form a corporation and draft a mission statement to explore and exploit a marketable concept. Then they sell—yes, literally sell—the incorporated concept to another person or corporation, one that has a deeper, more appropriately empowered position to turn the concept into achievement. Ideas have power. Ideas can and must be appraised—by positive-thinking experts.

Appraise the concept. Is it practical? Who needs it? Is it timely? Is there a market for the product or service? Can it be legitimately brought to the business table?

A dog-food company executive called his marketing and salespeople together for an urgent conference, because their product wasn't selling. Charts and graphs papered the walls. The latest marketing ads covered the table. Hour after hour, the meeting continued. Charges and complaints flew around the table, each department blaming another. Finally the CEO called on a meek and quiet little man seated at the far end of the table. "Joe," the CEO said, "what do you have to say? You haven't said one word or given one idea as to why we're facing such failure."

Joe gulped and then timidly said what no one else had dared to say: "Sir, there's only one reason. The dogs don't like the dog food!"

The appraisal of the concept has to address what's wrong with the idea. There's something negative in every positive idea. Every positive possibility will generate problems. Dreamers who fail to prepare for future shock are more often than not headed for a fall. List honestly and carefully the negative elements of the concept.

Is it possible to isolate, insulate, eliminate, or sublimate the negatives from the positive factors and forces in the concept? Is it possible to minimize the risk (or risks) inevitable through means such as these: insurance, a parachute, a lifeboat, a shield or a bullet-proof or lifesaving vest, a safety net?

What will it take to capitalize on the positive potential in the possibility? Calculate the insights wisely and courageously. Remember, though, that courage without wisdom and wisdom without courage both add up to a dangerous imbalance.

What's your idea really worth? Can it be sold? Are there enough people out there who want or need it badly enough to be motivated to change their priorities to reposition themselves to buy it? Now appraise your power base by checking your position in the all-important time management department.

Calendar. How much time will you need to implement this new opportunity? How young—or old—are you? Are the clock and calendar on your side? Your power will be based largely on the answers to these questions. In order to be successful, you've got to be able to say, "I've got a good idea—and the time to pull it off." Can you honestly say that? Remember that time is money and money is power.

Can you "rent," "borrow," or "buy" more time? How? Perhaps by reprioritizing the projects and persons who are drawing upon your limited time resources. By bringing in partners to participate. By offering an employee agreement to share proportionately the rewards of an eventual success.

Success or failure in the pursuit of a dream depends greatly on the power base of time.

Character. Your power to deliver on your potential rearrangement of priorities will relate closely to your personal reputation. Yes, if you hope to build your dream, you must first assess your character.

Are you believable? Can you be trusted? Are your word and wisdom reliable? Do you have the courage to make the commitment to follow through? Do you have integrity? If your answer to all of these questions is yes, you may already have more power than you think: if you pick up the telephone and share your new opportunity with powerful minds (backed by powerful money), you may find that your listeners encourage and support you, shifting a fresh opportunity from an impossibility to a real probability. Suddenly that opportunity moves from the bottom to the top of your priorities.

—∭—

Character = Power

—∭—

Top corporate chiefs whom I know and admire are men and women who are honest. They're not deceitful or duplicitous, and they're slow to work with promiscuous partners—even if those partners are talented and politically powerful.

"I'll never partner with an adulterer," one

CEO said to me. "If he'll cheat with his first love, if he'll lie to his wife, can't I expect that under pressure he'll lie to me or to my clients and customers? I cannot, must not, will not trust the person who doesn't have moral power in his heart of hearts."

That's good news for you! Build a reputation of impeccable integrity, and your power base will surely expand with amazing strength. Someone, somewhere will be attracted to you! You have a future.

I recall a supersuccessful person who, when seeking to hire important staff, would look to a few religious sects that had a reputation for insisting that their members live privately and passionately according to the moral standards and religious disciplines of the Ten Commandments. "I can't build a solid business unless my core people can be trusted," he told me. He rejected this popular rhetorical statement—"A person's private life doesn't matter if his or her professional skills are great"—because his experience had taught him otherwise. "In my book, no talent will ever compensate for a lack of trust," he concluded.

One of the tallest church towers constructed in the skyscraper era of the twentieth century can be found in earthquake-prone territory.

Called the Tower of Hope, it stands next to our all-glass Crystal Cathedral and houses part of our ministry. Both structures appear to be terribly vulnerable in this area of unstable soil. Yet they were engineered under the cautious eyes of two of this century's most respected architects: the architect of the Tower of Hope was Richard Neutra; the architect of the Crystal Cathedral was Philip Johnson. Both buildings have safely survived enormous earth tremors without damage. They shook, rattled, and rolled—but settled safely without injury to persons or property. The secret? Beneath the occupied structure of each building are powerful steel-reinforced concrete roots that hold down the foundations. Sixty-five-foot-deep holes were drilled through the shifting sandy surface soil to penetrate solid ground. Those concrete pillars are there forever! But they're intentionally out of sight. No one can or will ever photograph them. The glass and steel walls give the buildings quality and class. But the permanent, private power of the underground pillars of cement and steel gives each edifice character. You can trust those buildings. In the same way, our moral roots allow us to safely trust our lives in an apparently vulnerable environment. Those moral roots are the power base of our character.

Connections. How powerful is your base? Check your connections to find out. After all, there's considerable truth to the saying, "It's not what you know, it's who you know."

"How well connected are you?" That's a question you'll probably be asked repeatedly as you pursue your opportunity. So don't minimize your list of friends as you appraise your assets. Who will answer your letters? Who will take your calls? Who will accept your invitations? If you need a broader network, it's time to cash in on your character. Your well-earned reputation will pay off! You might be surprised at who will take your phone calls! Upgrade your self-appraisal.

You don't need more academic credentials if you can "buy" or "rent" the high-tech know-how from consultants who are in your particular business. There's a consultant out there who'd welcome you as his or her newest client!

There are talented financial consultants as well. You don't need to be wealthy to make your new opportunity fly; you simply need a creative financial package. Again, there are experts who can help you. So get connected, and get the power to smartly reorganize your priorities.

Cash. In estimating your power base, you also have to ask yourself, "Can I afford to

Courage
is
spelled
I-N-T-E-G-R-I-T-Y.

move on—or out or up or ahead?"

Whatever you do, don't impertinently ignore your power to put a grand new possibility on the top of your reorganized priority scale.

Short of cash? Check your assets. Some of them may have increased in value. You may be richer than you think. Reappraise them. Other assets may no longer hold the value to deliver the dividends they once promised. Perhaps it's time to cash them in and shift the investment to a new possibility.

How much cash will you need? When? Today, tomorrow, next year? Lay on the table your concept, your calendar, your character, and your connections, and you may discover that you can raise the cash with this power base.

You're coming close to making the decision to shift priorities in the face of fresh opportunities.

Competition. But before you make the move, reappraise your competition.

Is there competition? How broad is it? Has it cornered and covered the market? How strong is it? Can it easily and swiftly respond to your challenge and defeat you? Your power will be enhanced or diminished by the size, spirit, strength, and skill of existing or developing competition.

Getting ready to make changes in your priorities? But what if you're already positioned to move ahead with yesterday's priorities? What do you do? Pass on the new chance offered to you? Not yet.

Check Your Flexibility. Flexibility gives you the freedom to shift, shape, sort out, and settle on solid ground the foundation upon which your goals will rest. It gives you the right and the responsibility to recalculate the budget of your life's resources: time, money, energy, emotions, attention, and relationships.

It's time to pray. Take time to enter again the "soul room" in your mind. Here you must be totally honest and reflect on what you should place in the high-priority positions of power—the positions that control your life. Your decisions in this chamber will make or break you. Top priority? God and family, of course. Pour this priority in concrete. On this there are no decisions; it's a given.

In the rush of ideas, dreams, and hopes that stampede into your consciousness, to whom do you pay attention first? How about second and third? And what voice do you listen to before all others? You—yes, you—have become a celebrity, attracting an incredible crowd of ideas that press close to touch you. Some seek only a look. They seem to have a life of their own and aren't sure they want to be a part of your life—yet! Others want your attention, your time, your affirmation, your endorsement, your financial help. Many of these emotional impulses that invade your consciousness without invitation must be refused. Otherwise, they'll defocus you from being and doing what you're called by God to be and do.

PRIORITIZE THROUGH PRAYER

Your mind and memory system can easily become overloaded with and overwhelmed by too many competing options.

Is your collective consciousness like that disorganized, cluttered clothes closet we were rummaging through earlier? Do old habits still hang there? Tawdry old temptations? Didn't you decide to throw them away long ago? And here's a rod jammed with mental garments picked up back in cynical college days. Look at them! "Presuppositions" . . . "Preconceptions" . . . "Prejudgments." You were so sophisticated; you thought you were so smart when you bought them and brought them home to your emotional closet. But they don't fit or feel right anymore.

Your mental closet. Oh, God! Help me to organize it. Look what hangs in here! "Concepts" . . . "Compulsions" . . . "Invitations" . . . "Impulses" . . . "Assorted Assumptions" . . . "Addictions" . . . "Reactions"—all of this stuff jammed together, all competing for your recognition and respect.

But you stand in the secret dressing room of your mind and scan the scene. Check all the thoughts and the feelings inside of you. The hopes, hurts, dreams, and disappointments (social, spiritual, sexual).

In this secret dressing room of the soul, you stand—overwhelmed, confused, but excited—holding in your hand your newest "thing." A bright, beautiful idea! An exciting dream!

"Don't tell anyone," you whisper to yourself, "but look at this new dream! I want to go back to school and . . ." You hold the dream up in front of your imagination like a new garment you'd like to buy. You step to the full-length mirror. You turn to catch the side view. "This just might look great on me!" you think. A little fitting here. A tuck there. Can you afford it? Yes, if . . .

This is the decisive moment. This is the private power room where you'll secretly let your imagination try on a new dream.

This is the room Jesus talked about—the ultimate power room. He said, "And when you pray, enter into your closet, and when you have shut the door pray to your Father in secret and your Father who hears in this secret place will reward you—openly!" (Matthew 6:6).

What do you do in this secret room alone with your God who loves you?

Ask Him to help you choose what to throw away, what to keep. Some stuff is just shameful. He reaches for it, throws it where the trash will pile up; now He turns and smiles at you. "Isn't it fun getting rid of that!" He says exuberantly. "It didn't make you look good, really." He shuffles a few hangers.

"Now this!" He holds up and proudly shows you that beautiful and wonderful new dream. "This will bring the real beauty out in you!" He holds it in front of you. "Check this one. It's the real you!"

Suddenly decisive, you throw more of the tawdry, outdated stuff on the floor and reach for the new dream—one tailored just for you, tasteful, timely, and dignified! And you realize what a Savior God really is!

Possibility thinkers: pray and prioritize! This is where your life will take aim and find direction. Set priorities prayerfully. God is in-

A big
achievement
is made
up of
little steps.

spiring you. The Eternal Spirit is enlightening you. A beautiful new possibility is coming to your head and heart as a bright new hope! It's yours to wear. Perfect for the new you!

You've possibilitized. You've chosen a new dream. You've prioritized! Now you're ready to set goals! Make plans! Live a new life!

III

PLANS
MUST BE LAID

———〰———

R ecap. There are basically two kinds of
mind-sets in the human race. There are
negative thinkers and positive thinkers.
Put another way, there are impossibility thinkers
and possibility thinkers.

The poet Ella Wheeler Wilcox put it this way:

There are two kinds of people
on earth today.
Just two kinds of people
on earth, I say.
Not the rich and the poor
for to know a man's wealth
you must first know the state
of his conscience and health,
not the happy and sad.
For in life's passing years
each has his laughter

and each has his tears.
No, the two kinds of
people on earth I mean
are the people who lift
and the people who lean . . .

QUESTION: Why do possibility thinkers live such—what's the right word?—fulfilled lives, when impossibility thinkers live such empty lives?

ANSWER: Is it that possibility thinkers get brighter ideas? No, not necessarily. Impossibility thinkers often have the same so-called bright ideas.

REAL ANSWER: It's because possibility thinkers manage positive ideas, while impossibility thinkers mismanage the same ideas!

The process of success is almost scientifically systematized. And this systemic success is endemic—in possibility thinkers.

QUESTION: Isn't it true that possibility thinkers are goal-setting persons, while impossibility thinkers never set goals?

ANSWER: Not true. Both impossibility thinkers and possibility thinkers can pick up on the same positive possibility, and both can and may set goals. Yet impossibility thinkers fail in the end, while possibility thinkers enjoy success.

Why? For a starter, check out how smart people set goals.

THE PROCESS OF SUCCESSFUL GOAL SETTING

Successful possibility thinkers begin the process of goal setting by asking themselves three basic sets of questions:

1. **Is this a "goal-worthy" idea?** Does it weigh enough in value and worth on my values scale to merit considering turning the vision into a goal? (If the answer is yes, possibility thinkers move on to the second question.)

2. **Am I willing to add this idea to my list of priorities?** Would I be willing to rebudget my limited resources to cut this new possibility in at the appropriate level on my already scheduled list of "possible goals"? (If so, possibility thinkers move on to the next question.)

3. **Is there a game plan I can come up with to make this idea a success?** Even if it's impossible today, can I come up with

possibility-thinking plans that would allow me to turn this impossibility into a possibility? With some creative, innovative, progressive thinking, can this positive possibility be turned into a real probability?

Possibilities have been weighed. Priorities have been swayed. Now plans must be laid—all before irretrievable, irreversible, costly commitments are made! And plan-laying is what happens when possibility thinkers think their dareful, but careful and prayerful, way through the goal-setting process.

The place? Tachikawa, Japan. The year? 1969. I was a volunteer with the military, serving as the inspirational holiday leader during the weeks between Thanksgiving and Christmas for the men and women of our armed forces in the Pacific—Taiwan, Korea, Okinawa, and Japan. Now I was in Japan at the medical evaluation headquarters of the American military. A three-star general was briefing me. "We've lost only eleven lives in transit during the entire Vietnam War. And we owe that remarkable record to three words," he said, pointing to a sign that ran across one wall of the command headquarters. It read:

Check—Double-check—Recheck

"We studied the fatalities in World War II and the Korean War and discovered that many of the deaths had occurred while the wounded were being moved—by ambulance, helicopter, boat, train, or airplane. In all of our nation's major twentieth-century wars—World War I, World War II, and the Korean War—we'd assumed (and no one ever challenged this assumption!) that to get wounded to the next care station as fast as possible was always the smartest thing to do. In a desperate vision of cutting fatalities, we challenged that assumption in this war, and we discovered that the wounded person in transit is at special risk. In many cases it's best *not* to move the wounded, but to keep them stable, on the ground, until we can be sure they'll survive the next move.

"In all the previous wars, we usually checked vital signs, and if it looked safe, we ordered the person out—fast. In this war we do a preliminary check to see if they can make it on the next move. If so, we load them up on a boat or helicopter. But before that transport takes off, we double-check their vital signs. If the signs are still stable, we stay with the plan. The blades of the helicopter are whirling. But before we allow the helicopter to take off, we check the wounded person's vital signs for a third time. If everything is still okay, we're off. It's amazing how many lives have been saved in transit because the move was aborted after a double-check—or a final recheck."

There are always—in nearly every situation, anyway—so many variables, so much unpredictability, and so many uncertainties that smart possibility thinkers challenge their assumptions. They check, double-check, and recheck their priorities!

So you're exposed to a possibility? You've given it a great deal of thought and ranked your priorities? Good. Now recheck those priorities. You can step in or stay out? Think . . . rethink . . . search your soul . . . pray deep prayers. Let go and let God guide you. Ask the urgent questions!

In the world where I live and am accountable, what must be done before I check out? What must not be left undone?

What can I and only I do? What can I and only I deliver with integrity and excellence?

How much time do I have left? Time is something no one can replace. I've got to make changes in my lifestyle. How old am I? Sixty? Gosh, when I'm eighty I'll look back on how I spent the past twenty years!

When will the "window" on this opportunity close? The satellite is overhead now—but it's moving, and I'll soon be out of the window. The satellite won't slow down for me. Will it make another pass tomorrow?

How permanent will the negative impact be on my life's mission if I miss this chance? How temporary (or permanent) will the positive impact be on my mission if I succeed? Are we talking a "lease" or a "purchase"? "Rental" or "ownership"?

What does my power base look like today? How solid is it? Can a new move be made without exposing and eroding that base? If I succeed, will I stabilize and expand my power base?

What's the worst that could happen? Could I survive it? Can I design my own parachute? (What color? Green!) Can I start over again?

Can I design the exits? How? When? If it's not working, can I walk away without damaging my reputation, my integrity, and the really good people who respect me today?

Will I lose key persons because they disagree with my decision? Is that loss an assumption or a given? Can I live with that loss? Are they replaceable? Who and what are the persons or elements that are indispensable to my success? How long can I expect them to be around before I lose them by age or death or . . . ?

I'm interested in this possibility because there's a market. But is this my line of business? Am I in the position to be the right person at the right time to move on this?

Am I capable of putting my ego in its proper place as I challenge my presuppositions and my assumptions?

Can I and should I take the next step and "possibility think" plans that can be laid out successfully?

MOVING AN IDEA FROM A CONCEPT TO A COMMITMENT

At this stage of the goal-setting process, we're moving the idea from a concept to a commitment. Imaginative planning that connects a dream to a decision—that's what happens at this level. How does this process of possibility-thinking planning happen? That question is answered in the nine principles that I discuss below.

Principle 1

PLAY THE POSSIBILITY-THINKING GAME

I've given this advice for over forty years in my thousands of lectures to business leaders in Korea, Japan, Europe, Russia. I offered it at an all-day conference for over eight hundred young East European business leaders right after the Berlin Wall came down. And I've shared it in my books.

Start to play with the idea of success. Just play the game called possibility thinking. It's stimulating. It's safe. You haven't yet set a goal, after all. You've made no investment of energy, money, or reputation. Make it a game—but plan to win!

Calling it a game keeps the fear of failure

from coming into the subconscious, where it produces enough tension to block spontaneous creative thinking. A mental climate of genuine spontaneity releases a natural enthusiasm, which uncaps the subconscious forces that intuitively create really bright new ideas!

Turn the strategy of mental adventuring into a sport, thereby cultivating a creative mental attitude. Creativity happens when the subconscious knows it's protected from uninvited, pressure-producing interruptions.

The game? To come up with wild, wonderful, weird, amusing ways—what we might call possibility-winning moves—in which the impossible is mentally moved to the possible column.

Principle 2

CREATE TEN PLANS TO MAKE THE IMPOSSIBLE POSSIBLE

A plan is never a good plan.

"I've got a great dream, and a plan to pull it off." I've heard statements such as that often in my life. My usual reply is this: "You have a plan? Come back with plans, plural."

There's a rule in this possibility-thinking game that requires you to lay on the table at least ten ways to make the impossible dream

122

possible! You may include any hilarious proposal. It's a game, remember?

You can invite as many partners as you choose to come up with ideas. You need not stop with ten. When you're done, check the list. Take the one idea that stands out—agreed: it's great, if only it were possible. Now play the game with this idea—ten ways to make this idea possible!

You're on your way! You'll be in for surprises of creativity. I've played this game with every great impossible dream God ever gave me, and it's never failed me!

"Grandpa, how can I ever go to college with tuition so high?" Jason, a junior in high school, was busy poring over the college catalogs he had sent for, a disappointed frown furrowing his face. The prospect looked hopeless.

"Dad and Mom don't have that kind of money," he continued. "Besides, I have three younger brothers. Even if my parents could afford to send me to the college I choose, how could they possibly also send my brothers to the colleges they choose?"

"Now, Jason," I said with a hint of rebuke, "haven't I taught you to be a possibility thinker? Now's the time to use what I call my possibility-thinking game! I'm not making light of your challenge, but we have to release our creativity through the game. Let's try to make a list of ten different ways you can come up with to solve this college tuition problem. I think we'll both be surprised at the ideas that come out."

"Okay, Grandpa," Jason agreed, his frown transformed into a mischievous ear-to-ear grin. He picked up his pencil and started scribbling.

1. Let Grandpa pay the whole bill.
2. Win the lottery.
3. Get a full scholarship. (I'm pretty good at basketball.)
4. Get a student loan from the government.
5. Get a loan from both of my Grandpas.
6. Get a job and work my way through school, even if it takes longer to get my degree.
7. Sell my car. (That might pay for half a semester.)
8. Live on candy bars and milk. And take the jobs nobody else wants and clean toilets like you did, Grandpa.
9. Win an award or scholarship from Rotary Club, the Horatio Alger Association, or some other community club or corporation.
10. Join the Army, the Navy, or the Air Force and get my college degree that way.

What will be the result? I don't know, but Jason has started "possibilitizing" his way through college—of that I'm certain.

Principle 3

GIVE THE POSSIBILITY A CHANCE TO EXPOSE AND EXPRESS ITSELF

Let your dream expose its real potential. Every truly great idea has a life of its own. When such an idea enters the world of your mind, it's as if you were meeting a stranger for the first time. And this new acquaintance just may turn out to become one of the best friends you'll have in your lifetime. Think of your new dream as a living person, a being that wants to join up with you and bring its own circle of friends along.

Let that dream be invited into your living, breathing, imagination. The dream will begin attracting attention with its own magnetic power. Who's attracted to this idea? What "worlds within the world of worlds" does this dream fit into?

Every idea brings with it its own power. Give the idea a platform, introduce it to your friends, and see who's "turned on" by it and who's "turned off."

In my book *Move Ahead with Possibility Thinking*, published in 1967, I wrote: "Test the idea. Talk about it. If it's big and beautiful and impossible it will catch the ear of amazing persons you've never met. Support—and enthusiasm—will come out of the woodwork of this world. Be alert. Be aware. Be alive. The dream may be attracting the attention of someone who may have the secret, the key, the connection, to turn this beautiful impossibility into a possibility."

Principle 4

THINK LIKE A RENAISSANCE PERSON

"What's that?" you ask. I define the Renaissance mentality as an appreciation for creative insight, whatever its source. The true Renaissance person listens to and learns universal principles from many seemingly unrelated professions.

When I enrolled at Hope College in the year 1943, the president of that institution, Dr. Dimnent, taught my class in economics. He was also the architect of the great chapel. It was said that he was a "totally educated" and "completely learned" person. He was qualified by academic training to teach in any department—science, philosophy, language, art, and literature. He had never married. He was always reading, studying. He was the true "university" president. He could teach any one of seven languages. He could read original texts in German, French, Spanish, Greek, Latin, Hebrew, and English. He had a genuine overview of life, the mark of a true Renaissance man.

It is no longer possible for any person today to be a "completely learned" person. As accumulated, recorded knowledge has exploded worldwide, specialization in professions has gone wild! The more "learned" the "specialist" is in his or her "chosen field" the more ignorant and unlearned he or she will be in all of the other specialized departments.

We are one human family. All of us can and must learn from each other. Let science and religion learn from each other. Let the humanities and the healing professions learn from each other. Every department of life must see and envision how it impacts and is impacted by every other department! Ecology has taught us the unity of all of life in the universe: botany–plants, biology–creatures, zoology–animals, and so on. All are more interdependent in ways even Dr. Dimnent never understood.

The Renaissance mentality is another paradigm for creative thinking.

Imagine this scenario. A group of people from a variety of professions are talking together about issues relating to psychology. Suddenly a musician comes up with an insight: "Since tranquillity relieves tension, and that affects blood pressure, I find myself thinking, What kind of music generates tranquillity and what kinds of sounds generate tension?"

Now everyone listens! Even the medical doctor sees a connection unfolding.

A quiet man speaks up for the first time: "I'm an architect—actually, a specialist in landscape architecture. We've noticed that in landscape design, all plants are either dramatic or tranquil. Both have their place. But creativity happens when the mind of a person is relaxed, tranquil, in quiet peace. So plants as well as sounds affect the environment of peace."

Now a psychologist interrupts: "Yes, yes— we're onto something! I just had an idea: landscaping can be added to my therapy."

Another voice chimes in: "You know, I own a pet store. And what's happening in my market is that aquariums are "in" with dentists—yes, and lawyers too! The beautiful little fish float so peacefully through that underwater world that clients and patients waiting to be seen are relaxed just watching them swim." Possibility-thinking planning infused with Renaissance mentality equals creative breakthroughs.

PACK THE POWER OF OPTIMISM IN YOUR PLANNING

Optimism. Its potential power is explosive! My friend Dr. Martin Seligman is one of the world's leading pure research psychologists. It's his teaching that optimism isn't a shallow, unintelligent emotion. It's the energy-generating force in the human emotional system. Optimism is hope and hope is optimism. We all know where there's no hope there's no life; where there's no optimism, there is no future. It's that simple.

Where there is competition, optimism will mark the winner from the loser. The great contest for human thinking in the twentieth century centered in the competition between collectivism and individualism. When *Time* magazine chooses a "Man of the Year," the judgment is based not on "good or evil," but on the impact this person imposed on the whole world—for good or ill.

In this context I would name Nikolai Lenin as the "Man of the Century," for his revolutionary philosophy of Marxism introduced a new paradigm for addressing social problems. Enter collectivism: politicized and militarized under Lenin in Russia, global Communism became the threat of what became the "collectivist century."

Collectivism vs. individualism became the overpowering ideological battle of the century. The conflict invaded politics, economics, education, psychology, and religion. Both "sides" in conflicting ideologies were driven by optimism. Capitalism vs. communism; socialism vs. the free market; collectivism vs. individualism. The battle raged for most of the century. Only in the past decade—in the 1990s—did the Cold War finally end. Who won? Who lost? And why? The side that lost its optimism first—lost. The side where optimism was weakest—lost. That side was "Communism." Why did their optimism not match in power the optimism of individualism?

Recognize the power of optimism generated by one creative individual passionately committed to excellence.

For nearly forty years, people have heard me use this slogan: "If it's going to be, it's up to me!" And the collectivists have recoiled every time they heard it. They haven't, however, recoiled from the need for optimism. Yet the rugged individualist always generates optimism that's more forceful than the optimism generated by a compromising collective group. As a motivating force, optimism is most powerful when it's generated by one passionate, purposeful person dedicated to excellence.

In collectivism, optimism is based on communal sharing. But collectivists make a horrible error if they fail to see that optimism in a collective group is hard put to match the optimism generated by a creative individual. When a single unique individual is motivated to be a dynamic, creative thinker, he or she can outrun the group.

Optimism based on collectivism can't be committed to excellence, for collectivism can't survive without compromises. Collectivism requires unity of decision. That unity can happen only when attitudes are "averaged." This strategy inevitably moves from the individual's compulsion toward (and commitment to) excellence to the broader acceptance level of mediocrity. In other words, the cutting edge of excellence is dulled on the altar of cooperation.

Because the collective movement requires accommodating to internal political positioning and internal power plays, something less than excellence emerges in the compromise. The rare and rich details creatively envisioned and proposed by a solitary, dynamic leader tend to be voted down as fringe concepts by the majority. Subdued and silenced is the dynamic, energetic voice that's driven to excel with this positive compulsion: "If it's going to be, it's up to me!"

Thus maximum optimism is always generated by a gifted, talented, dedicated individual who is free to dream with an uncompromising commitment to excellence. To foster optimism, then, we need to empower and encourage persons to believe in themselves. A positive self-image, a strong self-confidence, a healthy self-esteem—these form the bedrock for a solid, healthy optimism.

Let's assume that you're that self-confident, dedicated dreamer, and you've got a bold new idea. How do you generate the optimism necessary to bring that dream to reality? You formulate a plan for success. Without that, the dream deserves to die. (No one wants to pursue a goal that won't and can't be a success.)

So no idea can be seriously and sensibly given a second thought unless and until some strategies for success with excellence can be outlined. Only then is true optimism born. Only then is optimism transformed into the truly awesome power of courageous creativity!

In the creative planning stage, optimism

must be the platform where ideas are expressed. An optimistic mental attitude is the admission requirement. The security alarm will go off when the pessimist steps forward. Have him stand back. Check him carefully. He may be safe—even helpful. But check him out carefully.

When and where and with whom does the optimist share his or her plans? There's danger here. The optimist needs to protect the plans from an early abortion or theft.

Caution: avoid sharing daring, adventuresome plans with neurotic pessimists who fail to pass the mental security check. Seek and select an intelligent collection of positive optimists— creative individuals committed to excellence.

The truly creative mind is easily repressed if a positive thinker knows that he or she needs the approval of a less motivated group of persons. The positive thinker knows how quickly a solitary smart suggestion can be overpowered by the collectively empowered fear of failure shared by a group of mediocre minds.

And with the onset of that fear, the motion to move ahead is lost. The negative votes add up to enough weight to swing the outcome of the election. The idea sinks under the collective burden of the fear of failure. The rare and risky plan is aborted before birth, and details of the rare and rich plan of the possibility thinker are never heard. What could have emerged and evolved as a bold and attention-getting proposal is deflected.

The overly cautious group then relaxes. They mistakenly assume that they've nipped the possibility of a failure in the bud. They've immunized themselves against the fear of failure in their addiction to negative thinking. The price they paid? The loss of a possible, progressive rebirth of enthusiasm and excitement that add up to dynamic optimism.

But let one imaginative possibility thinker be given the following—the freedom to dream a new dream, the encouragement to verbalize his vision, and the challenge to manage his imagination and conceive of (and lay out) the ways and means by which the concept could become achievable—and pessimism loses leadership. Optimism assumes power and control. The mental climate suddenly is charged with possible plans no one ever imagined before! Feel the power of hope fill the emptiness in the environment! The fatigue of pessimism is overcome by the fresh energy that optimism delivers! Positive plans laid on the table give a beautiful dream the chance to come alive!

Principle 6

THINK GLOBALLY; ACT LOCALLY

Be open to innovative thinking that intuitively taps into universal principles applying workable strategies in cross-professional and cross-cultural moves. True "success principles" aren't American principles; they're global and will work in the human family anywhere in the world. That concept is gaining wider acceptance with every passing year. The most shocking development in my life has been seeing how the "free-market" principles of success have become universally recognized and respected.

As you lay out plans at this stage of possibility thinking, think globally. All persons, all humans, all people—we're all basically the same. Never for a moment take your focus off this universal, elementary, success principle: Find a need and fill it! I'll repeat that principle—again and again—to keep us on target. It's the first lesson in success, and it won't be compromised anywhere in the world.

Every week I have to prepare messages that are delivered to millions of viewers in dozens of countries. I ask myself, "How will these teachings sound to thinking minds and human hearts in . . . Los Angeles, California? In London, England? In Johannesburg, South Africa? In Albania? In Moscow? In Siberia? In New Delhi, India? In Nazareth, Jerusalem, and Bethlehem? In Korea?" For many years, millions of persons have been a part of my weekly audience on global television. We try to find a need and fill it, certainly, but we also apply a second success principle: Think globally; act locally.

Which means . . . what? What are the deepest needs all humans face? One hundred years ago missionaries went to China to share the story of Jesus Christ and the positive Christian faith. My mother's brother, a Princeton graduate, went to be a missionary in China. But the civilization there reached back thousands of years. More than one religious philosophy had moved across that continent. How could my Uncle Henry get an audience? Find a need and fill it. He prayed, "Lord, help me to be truly helpful." When famine threatened families, he bought and gave rice to the hungry. His caring spirit was compelling. He was successful in getting a listening ear.

"Why do you give us this food?" he was asked.

"Because I'm a Christian. God has told me He wants to help people who are hurting. And a Christian is someone who says, 'God, use me to show Your caring love to the world. Here am I—use me.'"

So the missionaries did beautiful work. There was a medical doctor in every mission station, who brought the newest lifesaving medicines and offered frontline surgical procedures. Health-care institutions—that is, hospitals—didn't exist anywhere in that part of the world until Christian missionaries created them.

"Ten fingers for God," the missionary doctor would say, holding up open palms before he performed his operations. Think globally; act locally. The doctor recognized that in this Oriental culture parents had to sleep close to their children. So—having revealed his global thinking in his presence in the mission field—he acted locally and let the family sleep on the floor in the small "hospital room" whenever he bedded down a sick child.

Near the end of the twentieth century, I found myself to be a missionary to the world via global television. With all the contradicting philosophies, competing faiths, hostile religions, conflicting cultures, and warring politics, how could I possibly communicate successfully?

"Offer 'emotional rice' that will feed the hunger in their hearts"—that was the guidance

I was given by the God whom I love and seek to serve. Going back to my basic courses in psychology, I searched for the one universal need that marks the human being as a unique creature alive on planet earth.

What's the most basic need . . . desire . . . hunger . . . in the heart of a human being? I've posed this question often to the leading psychiatrists whose teachings I've studied. Searching for the answer, I felt led to the Bible, which clearly states that God "created the human being in His own image (Genesis 1:27)—and crowned the human being with glory and honor" (Psalm 8:5). This was it!

All humans are created to be creative. The fact that we were created "in God's image" means that all humans were designed to be "imaginative" creatures—that is, "faith-minded" persons capable of imagining that there's a Higher Power! All humans were created by this God to spiritually connect with the ultimate creative, cosmic, universal Mind called God, who wants to continue to be a Creator in the universe, using human beings in the creative process unfolding in society.

God wants to create hope, health, happiness, peace, and prosperity, at the hands of creative-thinking humans. Humans are creatures

that were designed to "think creatively"—
"think possibilities." And all of this leads to the
most satisfying prize the human could receive:
pride of personhood.

"Crowned with glory and honor." Wow! I
found it. Every human needs to feel honored—
not shamed. Pride of personhood—that's what
every person needs. The need for self-respect,
self-worth, self-esteem, self-confidence, self-
value—that's what every human being on
planet earth needs! And so I wrote a theology
of self-esteem.

I had discovered the "rice for hungry
hearts." I would prepare it in my own heart and
serve it, through television, to persons of all
races and cultures. That's where I am today.

———※※———

Think globally; act locally.

———※※———

Think globally. You can test any and every
possibility on this universal reality: humans
want and need to be honored and respected!
No product, philosophy, or service can ever
achieve success if it violates a person's hun-

ger for self-respect. This global spiritual reality mustn't be forgotten, violated, or abandoned in planning new projects and setting new goals.

So you have a dream? Plan the style, the spirit, the substance, and the strategy within the frame of reference we call self-esteem. So you want to sell a product? An invention? No one will buy it if it doesn't hold the promise of pride of ownership.

So you want to motivate persons to be lifted from the shame of poverty to the pride of prosperity? Then your plan of success must teach them to succeed by developing their God-given talents and gifts in such a way that they'll experience the pride of earnership even as they enjoy the pride of ownership!

So plans that are laid out must hold the hope of giving a human being the experience of the pride of belonging or the pride of becoming. Think globally; act locally!

Principle 7

LET POSITIVE ASSUMPTIONS MANAGE YOUR THINKING

At this early planning stage, positive assumptions are smart—not foolish. For you aren't yet making a commitment. You'll test the assumptions before you set goals.

But the core of possibility thinking is the mental activity we call "positive assuming." Even though the idea may have been unsuccessfully tried before, you should do the following:

- Assume that the times may have changed.
- Assume that nothing is as powerful as an idea whose time has come.
- Assume that there are solutions to the problems that have defeated the dream before.
- Assume that there are solutions to the money problems.
- Assume that costs can be cut, revenues can be increased, or the project can be refinanced over a longer period of time.
- Assume that smarter people can be either hired or invited as partners to make this challenging idea possible.
- Assume that obstructionists can be bypassed, isolated, or invited to join as partners in prosperity in a new joint venture.
- Assume that instead of a collision you could form a coalition!

Now you're exercising what religious people call faith. Faith is sometimes spelled A-S-S-U-M-E.

Negative thinkers and doubters will have a ready wisecrack: "That word is spelled ASS-U-ME." That's true only if a decision to make a costly, irreversible, risky investment is made on assumptions that aren't carefully and critically examined.

To allow negative assumptions to impulsively and impertinently discredit all possibility thinking at the planning stage is truly making an ass out of U and me!

At this early planning stage, you need all of the creative ideas you can get. And creative ideas won't proliferate if persons locked into negative assumptions are given a platform early on. There will be an appropriate time to challenge the viability of all positive assumptions. But at this planning stage, positive "assumption power" must be encouraged and applauded.

Let me introduce you to one of my heroes. His name is Robert Dedman. He was with me in the class of ten persons when I was elected into the Horatio Alger Association.

Bob was born in a simple country house in Arkansas. As a student in high school he had a dream. "Someday I want to be rich—very rich," he thought. He assumed that you could become very wealthy even though you had nothing at the start. It didn't cost him a dime to dream! So he shaped a stunning vision: "I want to be worth fifty million dollars when I reach the age of fifty. Then I'd love to give a million dollars a year to great causes in the world. If I could live to be a hundred, I could give all of the money away my last fifty years!" That would be fantastic—he assumed!

But "great dreams of great dreamers are never fulfilled—they are always transcended," the philosopher Whitehead said. How could Bob Dedman move from poverty to plenty? He assumed that he could become anything he wanted to become. Doctor, lawyer, merchant, chief. He assumed that law would be the smartest road to riches. So he became a lawyer. He did well. He was introduced at various clubs—and found that they were losing money. He assumed that he could cut costs, improve services, and turn losers into winners. He did just that. Soon other money-losing clubs noticed and asked for his help. He thought globally and acted locally!

By the time he was elected into the Horatio Alger Association, Bob's fortune had passed the fifty million mark many, many times. He'd been giving away a million dollars a year for many years. "Wouldn't it be fantastic to give a gift of fifty million dollars one year!" he fantasized. And he did it! Southern Methodist University was the recipient. His fortune has been estimated at the billion-dollar level, and he's planning to give it all away in his lifetime to medicine, education, community services, and positive religion. Focused on need, Bob Dedman is saved from greed! He's turned assumptions into achievements! He's my hero!

Principle 8

TURN CONTRADICTIONS INTO CREATIVE PLANNING

My exposure to superachievers has taught me that at every important junction of life, decision makers and planners encounter contradictions. Possibility thinkers must be prepared to turn contradictions into creative planning.

Jesus knew this, and He challenged us with this powerful paradox, this creative contradiction: "For whoever desires to save his life, will lose it" (Matthew 16:25). Likewise, the inspiring philanthropists I count as my friends all believe that it's impossible to give without getting much more back again.

Check out extremely successful business-

It's impossible
to give without
having it come
back to you. And
it's impossible
to keep what you
won't give away.

people. Their goal? To make a profit. Their secret? To conceive plans that hold the promise of giving more service, providing better products to the consumer at a lower price, and maximizing profit on the bottom line. Contradictions? You bet!

One of the greatest success stories in America's merchandising in the last decades of the twentieth century is the Nordstrom department stores. The architect and engineer of this stunning business success was a man I knew, loved, and admired, the late Jim Nordstrom. He took a solid business built by his father and insisted, because of his Christian principles, that the business deliver a product and service with generosity and integrity. With that as their foundation, Nordstrom stores earned a remarkable reputation. "If you're not satisfied with what you bought from us, just bring it back. We want only happy customers," he said. Anyone could simply walk back into the store, return the merchandise, and receive a welcome—a smile from the clerk and a "Thank-you for giving us your trust"—as well as a reimbursement!

"How did you dare to do that?" I asked him privately. "Didn't you have dishonest customers take advantage of you?"

He just laughed. (He was always laughing!) "Oh, sure," he said, "but even they came back to buy from us, because they knew they could trust us! And we got a reputation that brought customers in that you can't believe."

Contradictions! I've come to believe that when you dare to honestly, sincerely step in between contradictions, you have a fabulous opportunity to be creative.

Musicians know this. Minor and major chords play on each other.

Architects know this. Richard Neutra played the principle beautifully. He designed an altar made of poured cement. Once the wooden molds had been stripped away, wood grains were visible in the cement. Plaster and paint them? Oh, no! Leave them raw and rough—and lay soft carpet around their base.

Fabric designers know this too. They weave colors that clash and collide—pinks with reds and purples and greens. The contradictions are a setup for creativity.

Directors of drama and theater do the same. Silence on stage. The actor whispers. Now he shouts! Quietness—then the roar. Mountains meet valleys, and you've got a gorgeous view.

Athletes understand. There's no gain without pain.

Successful persons know it. There's no success without sacrifice.

At the planning stage, possibility thinkers let the contradictions challenge them. They're probably being set up for miracle thinking! They're ready to be creative and turn the dream into a goal! Because impossibility thinkers are always and immediately stopped by contradictions, you might become the pacesetter!

But before you make the commitment, consider one last principle central to this goal-processing stage.

Principle 9

IF YOU CAN BELIEVE IT, YOU CAN ACHIEVE IT

Now that's a positive assumption!

So you're planning. At this stage, omit the word impossible from your thinking and your talking. Think in "stages" and "levels" of achievement planning.

- **Starting plans.** Think about how you want to begin, how you intend to announce your intentions.
- **Short-range plans.** Try a thirty-day plan. A six-month plan. A one-year plan. You'll ad-

just your plans to your calendar as you rearrange both your priorities and your assets. You may have to sell some assets (real estate, stocks).
- **Long-range plans.** Five years? Ten years?
- **Now—think longer!** Twenty years? Thirty years? Forty years?

Almost always an impossible obstacle means only that you have to think longer. Nothing is impossible. Some things just take longer than others.

—⚋—

Think longer, think smarter, and think bigger—and you'll plan wisely.

—⚋—

Think longer. I was five years old when I got the dream of becoming a minister. The plan was laid. Eight years of preliminary schooling, four years of high school, four years of college, and three years of postgraduate work. Nineteen years! I call that my "twenty-year plan from a farm boy to a member of the profession of ordained clergy."

I was twenty-three years old when I got the dream of building a new church that would be big enough and strong enough to impact the "global market." I waited five years for the right time and place, knowing that I'd have to double my first twenty-year plan and create a new forty-year plan. The plan that was conceived decades ago soon became a goal—and today that dream has been transcended.

Think smarter. What elite doors could be opened for me by well-placed, power-connected people? I reached out to the world's leading religious thinkers—Billy Graham, Norman Vincent Peale, Fulton Sheen. I reached out to the world's leading psychiatrists—Viktor Frankl, most significantly. I reached out to the world's leading theologians—Samuel Shoemaker from America, E. Stanley Jones from India. I reached out to the world's leading architects—Richard Neutra, Philip Johnson.

Think bigger. Positive "assumption thinking" inspired me to think bigger. "Nothing is impossible."

As you read these lines, I'm practicing what I'm preaching. I'm weighing the possibilities, I'm swaying my priorities to give top priority in my remaining years to new mountainous, global, life-soaring goals that are being processed through my mind. I'm ready to go for it!

I've laid plans out on the table. May I share them with you? I hope they'll inspire you to reach out for the impossible dreams God is sending your way too! Nothing is impossible; we need only think . . . • longer • smarter • bigger.

At the age of seventy, I have a new twenty-year goal. To make the Crystal Cathedral Ministry one of the most powerful, positive, religious forces in the world for the next hundred years. How? By creating an endowment fund of one billion dollars! Today—it's impossible. So I'm playing again the possibility thinking game to achieve this impossible dream. Here I go!

Up to ten trillion dollars will change hands through wills and estates in the next thirty years. Some will leave huge gifts to medicine, art, and education. Ten percent might be left to religion—to our ministry? That's a possibility.

I have another possibility to achieve this apparent financial impossibility. To inspire one hundred thousand people to remember this ministry in their will for an average of only ten thousand dollars. Ten thousand dollars times one hundred thousand people equals one billion dollars! And thirty years from today there will be a powerful global ministry to motivate people to discover this ultimate truth: "If it's going to be, it's up to me!"

Nothing is impossible! I just have to . . .

• Plan longer
• Plan smarter
• Plan bigger

Remember: if you fail to plan, you plan to fail. So now, commitments must be made and the price must be paid.

IV
COMMITMENTS MUST BE MADE

———∞———

Y ou're about to set a goal. That's called commitment!

Possibilities have been weighed
Priorities have been swayed.
Plans have been laid . . . and now
Commitments must be made.

It's your turn to step into the exciting circle where the seeds of success germinate and sprout. Commitment! This is where your positive possibility leaves the womb, where your dream takes on a life of its own.

A commitment has three necessary components: vision, value, and voice.

• **Vision.** You have it. A dream has taken

form and shape, moving out of your fantasy into reality.

- **Value.** Your vision has profound value in your head and heart. You're willing to die for it.
- **Voice.** The newborn life utters its first cry. You make your commitment; you express your hopes. "Ask and you shall receive!" It's time to communicate your commitment to creative power-persons.

It's time to move from secret dreaming to open sharing. Connect with a carefully selected circle of positive-thinking friends, colleagues, and counselors. Share your dream honestly and openly.

But be wise: expose your vision only to positive-thinking persons. And be careful: never share a rewarding but risky vision with those who would have a conflict of interest.

Announce your intention to make a commitment to move ahead. Brief your wise advisers and counselors on the goal-setting process you're going through. Discuss how, when, and where you intend to begin and end. Explain that you aren't driven by irresponsible folly. Admit that your architecture of management has provided for exits, in case your colleagues advise you to detour your dream; explain your exit plans to reassure them. As you take these steps, know that the plans you're laying have moved the dream from a silent secret in your mind to the public decision-making phase.

Commitments must be made. That's where you are now.

Your mission statement will be honored if you make this first step: commitment. Your mission statement will be compromised, on the other hand, if you fail to commit to begin. So here you go!

GIVE YOUR DREAM A VOICE

The first step of serious commitment is giving your dream a voice.

Step one: you announce sincerely and with enthusiasm your proposed new goal. With this simple step, you've moved the concept out of thinking into talking. At this point it's only talk, of course, so the first level of commitment is still relatively risk-free. But you do invest a part of your reputation by exposing your intentions.

Now you've chosen an elite and select audience that can be trusted with what was a private, secret hope. This is a vulnerable hour of early exposure. Confidentiality must be ensured. You're part of a small power circle of trusted friends. You share the right ideas with the right people at the right time. You ask some crucial questions: "Is my feasibility study adequate? Are my insights on target?"

You announce your intended goal. You expose and express your confidence. You release openly, honestly, and fully your enthusiasm.

You express your impressions of the risks and the rewards in this possibility. You communicate the possibilities and the problems as you see them.

You solicit wise and constructive criticism from experts—perhaps lawyers, accountants, and other professionals. You ask them for their advice: "How far and how fast should I aim at this opening stage of goal setting?"

Their answers may run from A to Z:

Protect this secret dream until you're safe from "idea thieves." Go for a copyright, a trademark, a patent, a secured position, or a license.

We know of someone else who's onto this. Let him start and test the marketability of the concept.

Get the publicity jump and go public fast, with (1) a news conference, (2) a paper to be published in one of the specialized media, (3) a press conference, or (4) a legal document to secure your position.

Get another appraisal. Get another confidential professional opinion and see if it confirms your expectations.

Design an honorable exit if this first step reveals the need to shift to neutral or reverse, or to retreat.

At this stage, buying the whole idea could be too expensive [or ill-timed or unwise for a few—or many—reasons]. But to be intimidated to inaction may be a greater danger. So try to take over or buy an option, thereby giving yourself an exclusive agreement to proceed with due diligence.

<u>Step 2</u>

EXERCISE DUE DILIGENCE

The second step toward serious commitment in the process of goal setting is what I call "due diligence." Let me illustrate what I mean by that term.

Suppose you're making a commitment to buy a home. You've made your selection. That's level one of commitment. • You've made an offer to purchase. You've signed a purchase order. You've included a check as earnest money. And you've assured the sellers that you're serious. Now they can sell to no one else until you complete your "due diligence," which in this illustration consists of the precautions you take from this point on.

You aren't a reckless, irresponsible possibility thinker. You open an escrow account as a way to buy time while you get your act together. Before you make the irreversible plunge to close the deal, you put yourself in a positive position to spot and solve unforseen problems and challenges. There's still an exit before the commitment is final and the goal is firmly set.

You can check out the construction. You can confirm the numbers. You can recheck the appraisals. You can double-check and recheck your financial plan. If research during this "due diligence" level of commitment reveals discrepancies, you can exit with all of your money returned. But if all the details add up and the inspection is clear and clean, you can move to the next step in the goal-setting process.

Step 3

GRASP THE GOAL

The third step toward commitment I call "grasping the goal." With that third step, the goal is secured. You close the deal. You make the purchase. But what if your goal doesn't meet your earlier expectations? Do you quit? Walk away? Not yet.

What if the purchase of the house isn't satisfying? Then check your options and alternatives. Redecorate? Remodel? Relocate? Whatever you do, don't abandon the commitment you've made to own a home of your own.

I live in a house we bought twenty-four years ago. We had all five children by then. This small old house had only two bedrooms, though the attached garage had been turned into a third bedroom. The ambience of the home left much to be desired. My closest friends said, "What? You and your family would live here? Why would you buy this?"

My answer, all those many years ago: "I'm buying shelter, security, seclusion, and serenity. The house is on two acres of land—part of a hundred-year-old park. The trees are old, tall, peaceful. The entire garden is fenced and gated. My children can run and play safely there. I can put bright windows in the dark old walls to dispel the gloom and bring into the house the gladness of the garden. I can enlarge the house to add a bigger dining room, and later a music room, and still later a library and study for my work. I can't afford to do those things now, but I can afford new wallpaper, carpet, and drapes."

"What will you do with two acres behind fences?" I was challenged.

"Well, someday when the kids are on their own, perhaps with families of their own, I could break off two new lots—a half-acre on each side of our home—and these two families could enjoy the security, serenity, and seclusion of the private compound with us."

"But what if the three families aren't happy living so close together?" the friends persisted.

My answer: "Why wouldn't we all be happy with such safe and satisfying neighbors? We'd set rules. Each of the three homes would be on a separate legal piece of property. Anyone who chose to could sell and move. We'd all want privacy—but in a safe community. We'd telephone before we ran next door and interrupted a private family time. But in an emergency we could call each other anytime—day or night."

Twenty-four years later, that dream has come true. Today three families are happily living together in our private family compound. We simply apply in our private and public lives the positive principles of possibility thinking!

We have our two youngest daughters living

The path that can lift you from poverty to prosperity is around you— right now.

in their own houses on the free half-acre lots we gave them. Six grandchildren from these two families play in the enclosed garden-park we all share.

The path that can lift you from poverty to prosperity is around you—right now. Look! Think! Imagine! Believe! Get ready to set your goals. Because when firm commitments are made, goals will be set. And when commitments turn into goals, you're on your way to becoming more than you are today!

Ashima Mehta, another hero of mine, told her incredible story on the *Hour of Power* program. She was born in India—a country plagued with poverty. Even as I, at the age of five, had an uncle who inspired me with the possibility dream of becoming a minister, so Ashima had a grandmother who said to her little five-year-old granddaughter, "You should become a physician when you grow up: you could help so many people, and that would give you a happy life."

Then and there—when she was only five years old, living in one of the poorest nations on earth—Ashima Mehta was given the greatest blessing any person could be given: she was inspired by a fabulous dream, that of becoming a medical doctor! And instantly she made a commitment.

Then the war broke out. Muslims and Hindus battled each other. By the tens—no, hundreds—of thousands, death and casualties were inflicted horrifically.

"The enemy is coming. Run! There are trucks outside! We have to get out or we'll all be killed!" In that panicked scene, Ashima remembers someone picking her up and throwing her like a sack of sand onto a truck crowded with terrified women and children.

Where was her mother? Was she dead or alive? In the panic, they were separated. Would she ever see her mother again? She heard gunfire. She saw blood. Bodies of children were lying broken and bleeding on the road.

The truck quickly followed its long escape route, unloading at a distant refugee camp where Ashima would be found by her mother. No poverty pocket anywhere in the world of that day could be more pathetic than Ashima's. Refugee colonies in warfare—then as now—are where displaced, hungry, and diseased representatives of humanity huddle together in a desperate passion to survive one day at a time.

"I knew I would survive. I knew I was destined to become a physician. I would spend my life helping the children of the world —born and unborn." That's Ashima's testimony today.

How could she possibly dream her dreams in this horrific setting? How could she hope to get an education? How could she believe that she could make her dream come true?

One step at a time. She thought longer! Thought smarter! Thought bigger! Her goal was fixed—firmly, irrefutably—when she made that commitment with her overpowering faith in God. Ashima faced every imaginable obstacle with optimism.

Later, in medical school, she would meet the love of her life. They prayed for guidance after their marriage and were spiritually led to leave India for North America. They arrived in Canada with a total of only sixteen dollars— and no one to meet them and lead them to a place of employment. In a simple residence they found their first shelter, and in that foreign country they found employment. Then into Ashima's hands came the book *Move Ahead with Possibility Thinking*.

"Nothing is impossible if you keep the faith," she read. That statement bolstered her belief—in herself, in God, and in her future. And that book led her to listen to our television program every Sunday in Canada.

Dr. Ashima Mehta one Sunday opened her mind and met the greatest possibility thinker who ever lived: Jesus Christ. As she listened to our television program, she accepted Jesus as the face and form of the God who had called her as a child to become a physician. This newfound spiritual passion matched the commitment she'd made as a little girl to become a doctor. As a doctor, she now made a deeper commitment: to become a believer in and a follower of this positive Jesus Christ. Her feet were firmly fixed on the narrow path that leads to life—abundantly!

Today she and her husband live in Chicago, Illinois. Through her career as a pediatric physician, she joins with God in the miracle of saving newborn lives. Babies struggling to survive receive the miraculous help of her medical skill and dedication. Her husband? An oncologist who has established three clinics specializing in cancer.

"But isn't it depressing specializing in cancer patients when so many die?" I asked her husband.

"No, some are healed, and many live to inspire me," he declared. "I also find profound peace as God's servant as I bring comfort and courage to the dying."

"And," Ashima explained, "we use our income to bring faith into dark and empty lives. We couldn't live with the healthy remuneration we earn without giving back to God to bring the deeper, healing power of faith into our world."

As Ashima writes out her prescriptions, she often adds instructions to her patients to read positive books written by her television pastor. Today she and her husband underwrite the cost of delivering our positive-thinking Christian program to millions of television listeners in India. Her goals remain strong, unselfish, spiritual, and sincere. Ashima and her husband are superachievers. They've moved beyond success to significance, and beyond significance to satisfaction!

THE POWER OF COMMITMENT

The power of commitment is awesome in its reality!

Suddenly the Bible becomes profoundly scientific: God promises that if we have the faith, He'll reward us with the power!

Commitment power. How can you explain it? I've seen this God-inspired power released thousands of times when simple souls pray for guidance and make a lifetime commitment. Af-

166

I mmense life-giving energy is released when you've moved bravely and beautifully through the goal-setting process and dared to make a solid, sure, unshakable commitment.

ter forty years of specializing in possibility thinking, I can prove beyond doubt that commitment releases the greatest power a human can experience.

Where does the energy come from? From endorphins, yes. But what creative, cosmic power created a human brain capable of releasing such awesome chemicals?

I believe that the energy—the power, the zest, the vitality—is the presence of God within us.

Meet my friend Sam Moore. He's the publisher of Thomas Nelson Publishing Company, the world's largest publisher of Bibles.

He was born a poor kid in Lebanon. He came to America as a teenager with only a few dollars in his pocket. He couldn't get a job because many people didn't trust "foreigners." Sam prayed and practiced possibility thinking. He finally got a job selling Bibles door-to-door. He had a dream: he wanted to leave poverty behind and rise to prosperity. His first goal was to own his own car. Finally, after he'd saved seventeen hundred dollars, he went to the Chevrolet dealer with cash in hand.

"I want to buy that car," he said to the salesman, pointing to the lowest-priced new car on the lot. Smiling with pride, Sam held up the seventeen hundred dollars.

"That's not enough. You need more money than that," the salesman replied.

"Let me talk to the boss," Sam requested confidently. When the manager came out, Sam said, "You know, I want to buy that car. How much is it?"

"Seventeen hundred and seventy dollars. Lowest price," the manager answered.

"I've got seventeen one-hundred-dollar bills here for you." Sam held up the cash.

The manager looked at him, noting now that he was a foreigner and remembering his accent. "Where did you get that money?" he asked suspiciously.

Sam said, "I worked for it."

"Who hired you?"

He said, "A Bible company."

"A what?"

"Yes, sir. I sell Bibles."

"You didn't earn that money selling Bibles!"

"Yes, I did."

The manager was still suspicious that this customer was a crook. "Let's see one of those Bibles you sell."

Sam reached down into his briefcase and pulled out a sample. "Look at this Bible. This

169

is a great Bible." Sam got so enthusiastic pointing out the features of that particular Bible that the manager replied, "My goodness, I never did see a Bible like that. That really is pretty nice. How much is it?"

And Sam sold him the Bible! Then Sam said, "You know, you ought to get a separate Bible for your wife, because she probably reads at different times than you do."

"You know, that's not a bad idea," the manager agreed. "I'll take another one."

One of the other salespeople, watching the scene unfold, said to his boss, "You ought to give one to the top salesperson of the year."

"Good idea," the manager said. "You know what? I think maybe we'd be better at our business if everyone who worked here read the Bible. Do you have four more?"

By the time Sam was finished, he had enough cash to make the purchase. He drove off in his new Chevrolet!

Meet another friend of mine, this time from Hong Kong. Sam Yung found so much inspiration in the Chinese translation of *Move Ahead with Possibility Thinking* that he connected with me. Nearly thirty years ago his father and mother fled mainland China and became refugees in a horrific, pathetic, dangerous slum in Kowloon. That's where Sam was born. Five persons—he, his dad and mom, and two other siblings—lived in a room only seven feet wide and ten feet long—seventy square feet! They ate and slept there for five years. Then Sam Yung's father saved enough to move his family into larger quarters—but still only a hundred and fifty square feet. And the dwelling was still in a slum jammed with refugees. Sam's young friends? Many, many of them would become sick, die, or turn to crime and be killed or sent to jail.

Something miraculous happened to Sam. At the age of sixteen he heard that God exists. That He came to this earth and lived in the person called Jesus.

"I like that," Sam said. "I can believe that. I'll buy that." And Sam made a very important commitment—the first of many commitments he would make. He became a passionate Christian at the age of sixteen. He loved the Bible, with all its stories about Jesus. Then he made a second commitment: "I'm going to work hard." He began to set specific goals as well: "I'm going to become a rich, committed Christian," he vowed. He worked hard in school. When he graduated from high school, he got a job as a clerk in a bank. There one of his special clients mentioned life insurance.

"Life insurance, what's that?" Sam asked.

The man explained, adding, "You really ought to be a salesman. Sell life insurance. You don't need any money to sell life insurance."

So Sam decided to become a life insurance salesman. That goal became his third commitment.

But Sam recently made still another commitment: to give something back—generously! He's Christ-motivated!

Today he's a very active volunteer on the committee of the United Fund. His personal target is to raise two million dollars to contribute to the United Fund in 1996. At this writing I do not know if Sam has reached his goal, but I was not surprised that the Chamber of Commerce of Hong Kong selected him as one of the ten outstanding young business people in Hong Kong. Yes, he's become a great success!

He recently visited America as a member of the Million Dollar Club.

"Sam, where do you live now?" I asked him. "You were building a house when I was in Hong Kong a couple of years ago."

"Yes," he said. "It's finished."

"If I wanted to buy it," I asked, "what would it cost me?"

"In American dollars?" he asked.

I nodded.

"Between six and eight million," he said, calculating the exchange rate in his head.

Wow!

He said, "I built this fabulous home so I could invite all of my rich clients to have dinner at my home. . . . Whenever clients come for an evening, we have a fabulous dinner in a gorgeous setting. Then I tell them about Jesus Christ. Many of them accept Jesus Christ, and I baptize them in my swimming pool. I've got a beautiful swimming pool. I don't swim; my wife doesn't swim. It's really my baptismal pool."

That's Sam Yung. He started with an "invincible surmise": "I'll become a rich Christian."

Just look where this commitment led him! From surmise to success: from success to significance: from significance to spiritual satisfaction. Now that's abundant living! That's prosperity that delivers real pleasure with humble pride!

The power of a commitment. It's reality—not mere rhetoric. It's incredible! What is it that gives a dream so much power?

This could prove to be the most important chapter in this book.

The lessons I share here could be the most challenging words you'll ever read.

Life or death—that's what depends on how seriously you read these sentences. If you receive them in a cavalier spirit, be prepared: the landing gear will come down prematurely and you'll descend to earth. Read them sincerely, and you'll gain altitude and go for a longer flight than you've ever imagined.

The first three chapters were safe. This chapter, though, brings you to the point where a decision must be made. You—and only you—can make that decision. It's called commitment. And commitment will demand from you the personal responsibility to set goals.

The success process will move on from here—from reflection to action. Set goals—and live. Avoid them—and the slow but certain seeds of dying will invade your life.

Believe me: I know! I had to reach the age of seventy to learn how dangerous and potentially disastrous it is to have no goals. After all, I've lived all of my life under the domination of glorious goals.

Because I was goal-dominated, I was alive with enthusiasm when I turned thirty, then forty, and then fifty.

When I turned sixty, I could see that before I hit seventy I would have fulfilled my forty-year goal. Then what? Retire at the age of sixty-eight? I sensed a gradual drop in the level of my enthusiasm for living. I survived, to be sure. But I felt the emergence of a foreign feeling I could define only as "growing old."

My sixty-ninth birthday was a tough one. I felt as if I'd lived my life. No longer was I a goal-oriented person. I'd never before experienced life lived in that vacuum. I shared my emotional emptiness on that grim birthday with my wife. I'll never forget our tearful talk that morning in our kitchen.

"Bob, you must find and set a new ten-year goal and be prepared to extend that to a twenty-year goal. Your problem is a temptation to yield to a life that's free from the pressure of commitment to goals. Set new goals and live—or retire in self-indulgent laziness. But if you choose the latter, you'll die—too young!"

"But I can't imagine any new, challenging,

and more exciting goals at the age of seventy!" I protested.

"Listen, Bob, set a goal of writing a new book."

"But I've said it all!" I argued.

"No, you haven't," she insisted. "You haven't written a book that includes lessons people never learn until they reach the age of seventy! And Bob, you've achieved your goal of building a great church. It's paid for. No debt. But that beautiful power base for spiritual motivation won't survive the coming decades and centuries without a strong financial base. The hundred-million-dollar facility is debt-free, but it isn't endowed. It must be. Or trees will crack the curbs, weeds will replace flowers, windows will break. In times of economic recession, the entire beautiful base you've spent your life creating will crumble. Your job isn't finished. You have a responsibility to secure your success by setting new goals to meet these inevitable needs that the next century will impose on your achievements." She added, "Pray about it. Don't listen to me; listen to God."

Deep in my heart I was struck as if with a sword from heaven.

But that next year was my toughest. I fought the commitment. I recoiled in the face of new and challenging goals. I kept praying—but vacillating too. I wouldn't set goals! And I lost my youthful energy for the first time in my life.

On the eve of my seventieth birthday I gave orders to my wife: "I don't want a birthday party. Please!"

The dreaded day arrived. My son told me he'd been honored to be selected as one of the top ten "young leaders of tomorrow" by an Orange County community club. Would I attend the dinner and introduce him?

Yes! I loved the idea.

"It's a black-tie affair, Dad, okay?"

"No problem," I answered.

"Meet me in the hotel lobby and we'll make our entrance together," he suggested. I agreed.

We followed arrows directing us to the ballroom. At the door was a sign that read, "Future Leaders' Banquet." I was so proud of my son! I still had no suspicion that it was all a hoax.

As he opened the door, a packed ballroom of people leaped to their feet and shouted, "Happy birthday, Dr. Schuller!"

I was blown away. It was a surprise birthday party for me. Over two hundred of my closest family and dearest friends were there! They came from across America. I'd never had an experience like it, and probably won't again.

I can best describe my feelings as being ravished by the love of God. I could hear a silent whisper in my ear that I sensed was a message from Jesus Christ himself. (He's been my best friend all of my seventy years.) I heard him whisper, "Happy birthday, Bob! And do I have a gift for you!"

Then and there I caught a new vision, with value and a voice! I couldn't believe the power in that room. Good people. Great friends. Loving family.

"Look around you, Bob, and get ready to set new goals—the greatest goals you've ever set! And I am with you always!" Those were God's words to me. I listened. And I started my seventh decade determined to (1) publish a new book (you're reading it now!) and (2) keep good news on global television through the next century. My goals are set! I'm once again living a goal-managed life.

Now, let me tell you—I'm young again. I feel as if I were only forty years old. I'm driven with a new passion. I'm astounded at the youthful energy and fresh enthusiasm I feel as I plan the next ten and twenty years of my life.

What I've learned at this amazing age is how goal setting releases unbelievable power into human personality. So I can write here what I've just learned from personal experience. I've never before written (or read elsewhere) the lessons on the pages that follow.

I'm terribly excited to share with you the honest-to-God truths I've learned!

HOW GOAL SETTING IGNITES HIGHER POWER

After a lifetime of research I'm prepared to share the following twenty reasons why a committed goal generates incredible energy:

1. When you set a goal and make a commitment, **a decision is made** that plugs the holes in your personality. Indecisiveness allows a lot of energy to be drained out. Wasted!

2. When the commitment is made, **enthusiasm is released.** That commitment uncorks the powerful energy of your soul, no matter how young or old you are. Committed goals tap the powerful emotions of deep enthusiasm! The Greek words *en-Theos* are translated "in God." From that derivation comes the English word enthusiasm (as well as its Russian equivalent).

3. When the challenge is accepted, **you're released from apathy,** which blocks the release

Goal setting
releases
unbelievable
power into
human
personality.

of unbelievable emotional energy.

4. **Excellence is targeted and marketed.** Mediocrity, which stifles the flow of energy, is rejected. Excellence becomes your mental fix and generates incredible passion—in other words, power! When you know that what you're doing is better than anything that's ever been done before, the power that's released is astounding.

5. **Leadership is asserted.** You're king, and you know that you're in control of your life and your future. You realize that you have control! Power? It's there! Immediately. Drive? You've got it!

6. **Faith is put in control of your future.** Possibility thinking is in command, and that releases a deep spiritual strength. Now you're aware, awake, alive, alert, active, aggressive! The generator of energy is turned on. The brownout is over. Power returns!

7. What gives so much power to a goal-setting commitment? Just this: when you're committed to goals, **you feel free to become more than what you've done, free to become more than you are.** Suddenly you truly are free! The commitment to your dream liberates you from the energy-blocking prison of ambiguity, indecision, and confused priorities. You're free

to run and strive. Try to imagine the energy that comes into the body of the Olympian when the starting gun goes off.

8. **Hope is renewed; optimism blossoms.** You believe you just might succeed. But you know it's always more than you can pull off alone. You know you cannot and must not fail, so you are humble enough to ask God for help.

9. **You become a spiritual person, a God-connected human.** You connect—knowingly or unknowingly—with forces that release a spiritual passion and drive. Why does commitment release such power? You know that success isn't possible if you don't set a goal. And now that you've set a goal, you need all the help you can get. That's a setup for God to move in. You may have prayed as a child: "Dear God, help me to be a success. Please don't let me fail." God doesn't forget that prayer once you've sent it to Him. And if your goal was conceived in prayer, where does that lead? To God. God is now given the chance to control your life. A goal-managed person becomes a God-controlled person.

10. **Personhood is affirmed** when you make a commitment to your goal. You've made a decision; you're committed to a new goal. You have God's attention. Now you're no longer

It's a spiritually scientific fact: fresh dreams turned into committed goals generate immense power!

intimidated by peers or manipulated by society. You're managing your life, under God's watchful eye! You're no longer a product, a puppet, a computer. You're a person! The power of personhood surges within you!

11. **Success is honored and ensured.** For when you commit to a goal, it's impossible to be a total failure. At least you've succeeded in taking command of your own destiny! You've broken free from the antisuccess mental attitudes that are all around you.

12. **Direction is established.** I can't tell you what a collective loss of energy results when people don't know where to go or what to do. Traffic really slows down when you follow a driver who doesn't know which street to take. Direction blocks the leaks caused by ambiguity.

13. **Fears are overpowered.** Oh, they're not eliminated. In fact, since you've committed to a goal you've gained some new fears, I'm sure. But your fears are overpowered. Your response to fear is this: "I'd rather attempt to do something great and fail than attempt to do nothing and succeed." You can feel more energy flowing deep within you.

14. **The focus of your life is fixed.** This focus enables you to plug any remaining holes

from which energy is leaking out. Water that flows unfocused becomes a swamp. What a waste! There's no forceful energy in a swamp. But water that's channeled into river banks, pipes, and conduits generates immense energy and force. Resources—emotional resources, time resources, money resources—are now generated, managed, and controlled!

15. **Opportunities are given a chance to become achievements.** Opportunities aren't even given a shot at success until you commit to a goal. They don't wait for you. They never do. They never will. Opportunities are on the hunt—looking for someone who will recognize, respect, and reach out for them. Someone else will grab them if you don't. Sorry: if it's not you, the next person watching and waiting in line will make it happen.

16. **Youth is renewed.** Yes, I really am seventy years young! I've never felt healthier or stronger or more enthusiastic about the next ten years at any phase of my life. Age isn't a matter of calendar; it's a matter of what your head is filled with. If you've got dreams, you're alive. And if you don't—I don't care if you're fifteen or fifty—you're going to be dead and bored and seek stimulation by resorting to drugs or sex or self-indulgence or sin. What a

waste of potential excitement, adventure, and enthusiasm!

No doubt about it. When you set goals and make commitments, you release enthusiasm. You generate energy. You plug the holes where fatigue leaks in and pollutes your personality! What does that mean? Endorphins go to work. You're energetic, enthusiastic, creative. You live rather than die. Have you noticed that many people don't live long after retirement? Why is that? They die because the energy isn't there. And the energy isn't there because the enthusiasm isn't there. And the enthusiasm isn't there because those retirees don't want to make any more commitments to goals. They've surrendered to laziness and apathy. They think that they're relaxed and feeling good because they don't have the pressures of commitments, but that dangerous and deceptive freedom blocks the flow of endorphins through the brain.

Youth is renewed when we set new goals. We can't live—truly and vibrantly live—without them!

17. **Relationships are expanded and empowered.** Every time you commit to a goal, you're being set up for new connections. Your power circle is bound to change. Some people will no longer be important in your power circle;

new names will show up on the roster. Your whole circle of relationships will change. And if you prayed for a goal and committed to that goal, energy will come from the encouragement and support of new friends. People will come out of the shadows. Your new goal will attract attention from people you've never met.

The power of a committed dream—how it changes your relationships! I was born on a very poor Iowa farm. Our family was not in the "social " circles. I can't tell you how humble I feel to know the people I know today. Wonderful people. Powerful people.

Set a goal and commit to it! It will attract attention. You'll get a letter, then a telephone call. People don't attract attention, but powerful ideas surely do! I can't tell you how many people I know, how many friends I have. How did I get connected with those friends? My commitment to the dream and the goal of trying to make a better world through positive thinking has drawn power-people from the wings. Somehow the right people have always been in the right spot, offering the right help at the right time. Success won't happen until wonderful people are attracted to your goal and make you the success you were meant to be.

18. **Your power base is broadened.** Sud-

denly you are standing on a power base that is stronger, more solid, broader, and deeper.

19. **Your priorities are concretized.** Goals are written now in ink, no longer in pencil. Better yet, carved in granite rather than scratched on a piece of paper. When you make a commitment to your dream, you put your priorities in cement. And God alone knows what energies are going to be forthcoming. Determination is a volcano!

20. Why does commitment to a dream generate such power? **Your vision is crystallized!** Your private secret is exposed! Fantasy becomes reality. The idea now has legs and wings.

The dream becomes a diamond. It attracts attention. Persons known to God (but unknown to you) will take notice, attracted to the beautiful new flash. It's God's way of answering your prayers. Support! Strength! Success! They start like a stream and become a river—flowing to you!

So set your goal and be prepared to go for it. That's called commitment! Once you've committed to a goal, the power will begin to flow into your life.

The Atlanta '96 Summer Olympics are beginning as I write this. I've just held in my hand a veteran Olympic torch. My daughter Carol earned and owns it. It's made of brass and leather. Carved in the brass are these words: "Games of the 23rd Olympiad, Los Angeles 1984." She carried this torch running on one leg. Circling the top of the torch are three words—words that represent the theme of the Olympics: citius (faster), altius (higher), and fortius (stronger)!

Carol carried this torch painfully but powerfully not long after her leg was amputated. Though she would never be an Olympic athlete, she was and is a success. She carried the torch and held it high, her hair flying in the wind. What energy! The pride of who she is and the goals she's committed to gave her an energy and spirit that few "normal" (as she would describe those of us who have two legs) people ever tap into!

It's commitment time! It's time for you to grab hold of the torch. God wants to hand it to you. Take it, and see what God can do with the life you've got to live.

The power of a committed dream. You're there! You're moving into the mental power circles where dreams are waiting to be embraced with your "aha!"

You've made a commitment!

Now be prepared to give your dream all you've got!

V

THE PRICE
MUST BE PAID

—〜〜—

My friend Quincy Jones was the well-applauded producer of the 1996 Oscars. Quincy was raised in poverty in Seattle and today he is a super success. Shortly after the Oscars I asked Quincy, "I'm writing a new book. Any lines in your memory that have been a steady inspiration in your life?" His eyes twinkled and out came these lines:

"Once a task has just begun,
never leave it 'til it's done,
Be the labor great or small,
Do it well or not at all."

Success demands that we pay the price excellence demands. The price always calls for sacrifice. Goals that are always and only self-serving never deliver satisfying success.

So now!

By this time you've made life's most urgent commitment: You've set new goals. They are meaningful, measurable, and manageable.

Meaningful Goals. They were weighed carefully and prayerfully in your mission statement. They have come from your passion to find a need and fill it . . . focus on a hurt and heal it . . . confront a conflict and resolve it . . . challenge a problem and manage it . . . spot an opportunity and seize it.

In short, your goals crystallize your values. In your goals you've discovered and exposed the real you, the person that you really are! But are your goals worth the price you'll have to pay? Achieved, they could make a marvelous difference in many lives besides your own. Now you need to be prepared to pay the price attached to them.

Measurable Goals. Results and rewards must be recognizable and quantifiable all along the way. For that reason, it's helpful to have several categories of goals: immediate, short-range, and long-range.

The major long-range goal may be fixed clearly in your mind, a strong beacon. Even so, you must have some shorter-range goals that allow you to see some progress—soon! This is essential.

Steps—however short and slow—must be taken to keep the hope alive. A college degree? Finishing high school is a good first step. Then apply to a college. Rejected? Fix the problem by taking a review course or doing volunteer work in your chosen field. Then try again. You can and will be accepted if you keep on trying. And keep measuring what you've accomplished. You're building a base; and reassured of eventual success, you'll be motivated to keep on paying the price—one step at a time. You're progressing! You're moving ahead!

Never lose sight of your long-range goal. But you must break that big task up into short- and intermediate-range goals. The human spirit needs the constant encouragement that comes with achievements at primary, and then secondary, and then advanced levels.

At each level you'll be reassured that you've earned another dividend from your commitment and your latest investment. And you'll keep on moving ahead, knowing that inch by inch, anything's a cinch. You're simply paying the price.

Manageable Goals. What's your long-range goal? Perhaps to be professionally certified? Financially secure? Whatever your ultimate goal may be, you're in a command position to manage your development to achieve ultimate success.

Management is the decisive control of the expenditure of resources to maximize productivity. Good management minimizes the waste of your assets—your heart, your time, your purse, and your talent (which includes knowledge, skill, and training).

A great goal is like a beautiful old-fashioned wristwatch. The watch is made up of numerous items—spring, gears, hands, dial, and a case that packages the pieces to make a useful and attractive product. Goals too can be broken down into intricate components, which is why goal management is so crucial.

But how do you manage goals? How is it done? The answer lies in a simple formula: Decide—then divide and conquer! Let's look at what that means.

Walter Burke was president of McDonnell Douglas when President Kennedy called to tell him the goal was set: "We're going to put a man on the moon!"

"Dr. Schuller," Walter told me, "I knew that was impossible. But if we were going to do the impossible, we had to ask what made it impossible. So we took the goal and saw that it was a collection of many problems. We carefully analyzed and dismantled the 'big problem' into all the separate problems. When we looked at all of the separate problems, they made that ultimate goal appear to be one impossible problem.

"Then we went to work—assigning the variety of small and larger separate problems to the right places and persons, directing each person to solve only the one problem we handed to him. So problem after problem was handled. One solution at a time—like a puzzle coming together. By the time we had only one unsolved problem left, so many people had made such a large accumulated investment that quitting was simply out of the question! 'I found it!' The last piece in the puzzle. That's how we felt when it all came together."

Walter Burke taught me the engineering principle of Decide —then divide and conquer. Big problems? I no longer believe there's any such thing as one big problem; I've come to see that every problem is a "wristwatch." Take it apart. Analyze it. It's a collection of challenges. See your problem as separate pieces to be handled one by one! You'll be astounded how you can recognize, research, and resolve them. You're now the manager of your goals!

Now you stand at the ticket window. The cashier asks, "Do you want to purchase a ticket to move ahead? Or do you want to go back?"

A price must be paid!

Actually, you'll pay a price whatever you do. Even the quitter pays. You can't walk away from your dream without paying a price. The fatigued, frustrated, burned-out dreamer can't exit without buying his freedom to walk away. The price you'll be called to pay for abandoning your goal is living without the rewards that you might have earned and enjoyed had you paid the price to move ahead.

The bottom line? We pay a price for both rewards and regrets.

Choose to purchase a fruitful and fulfilling future. Gladly pay the price that offers the greatest possibility of personal pride. Pay the price to succeed, or pay the price to fail—it's your choice.

Before you pay the price, reassess your commitment and reappraise your goals.

Check, double-check, and recheck your potential for survival and success.

Before you write the check, ask the following smart questions. (You say you already did? Well, recheck!)

1. Who needs it? What good will it do? Is there a legitimate market for my goal?

2. What are the nonnegotiable parameters I must meet? When the decision was made in England and France to abandon building the *Concorde* after billions of dollars had been spent, that plane's builders blamed TWA for not picking up their option to buy a large number of planes. "Don't blame us," they were told. "It uses too much fuel and has too few seats."

3. If I pay the price to succeed, will I really build something of real value? Like—

- An education
- A career
- A business
- A profession
- A marriage
- A family
- An organization
- A structure
- A piece of artwork or craftwork
- A new relationship
- A reputation

4. Or is this primarily an ego trip for me? People are rightfully suspicious of (and slow to support) another person's ego trip.

5. Am I driven by hunger? Do I have passion—a deep desire, a burning drive? I'll need that! The price in emotional terms may be very heavy.

6. Am I driven toward this goal by a compulsion to excel? To improve? To create or innovate? To contribute to human progress? Or is this perhaps an emotional purchase motivated by boredom?

7. I can't be sure of my success. Risk is involved. If I fall short of my goal, how can I exit? Is there a parachute? Can I start over again? Will I be able to take something positive away with me—something beyond the scars and blank checks? Like—

- A reputation for integrity or courage
- Experience that translates into further education
- New relationships and stronger friends, who will respect and applaud me for trying

8. Will this goal—pursued and achieved—make me irreplaceable in the market of human endeavor? My friend John Teets, CEO of the Dial Corporation, says, "Make yourself irreplaceable!" Whatever I do—whatever I become—can I excel? In the market of human employ

ment, can I be a little better or smarter? More honest? More dedicated? More loyal? More dependable? More generous? Kinder? More positive and pleasant?

I think you're ready to appraise your investment, pay the price, and give your dream all you've got! Let's do it!

"Everything that's nice has its price." That's a line all five of my children have heard (and learned) many times. All of your resources will now be called for to turn your goals into a solid, base-building achievement:

Let me draw three pictures for you to fix in your thinking:

1	2	3
The heart	The clock & calendar	Money

Yes, be prepared to pay the price of success. There will be demands:

- On your emotional resources
- On your time
- On your money

When you made your commitment and set your goals, the seeds of success that you planted sprouted. You can feel it!

Your dream was conceived in the womb of your imagination. When you set goals, your pregnancy culminated in delivery. The dream was born and now has a life of its own! Like every new life, it cries and calls for food and nourishment. And you cannot, you must not, you will not let the dream die!

You're the caregiver of a new life. You'll hear its call for help and feed it, care for it, and protect it. You'll gladly pay the price—in heart, in time, and in money.

Price 1

START WITH THE HEART

Passion is the key to success. Every achiever I've met is quick to admit that the passion for his or her dream made it happen. But the price you have to pay must start with the heart.

Marcus Aurelius said it well: "Remember that what pulls the strings is the force hidden within; there lies the power to persuade, there the life."

There's no doubt that emotional resources are the first and most important investment you'll be asked to make if you want to be led to honorable accomplishment. From start to finish, your heart will be called on to fuel your pursuit. High achievers are marked by deep emotional power—the power to be flexible, adaptable, accommodating, adjustable. Patience drains emotional energy. You'll need plenty of energy! Do you have it?

Yes, every project demands payment from your emotional reserves. As a precaution, fill your emotional fuel tank before you take off. As I write these lines, the evening news has just reported a plane crash in Burbank, California. A pilot landed his private plane at the Burbank airport, picked up his father and mother, took off again promptly—and crashed only moments later. All three passengers were killed. But there was no fire! How could that be? When inspectors noticed the absence of gas on the ground, they checked the gas tanks. Dry. Incredible! Witnesses say that the pilot was in such a hurry that he didn't take time to fuel up before takeoff.

Don't make the same mistake. Fuel up before takeoff. Start with the heart. The natural enthusiasm released with the commitment may be enough for takeoff but not adequate for the long trip you're planning. You must be prepared for storms, detours, and delays, your heart filled with enough spiritual fuel to keep your positive passion tuned in to optimism and enthusiasm. Without heart-power, emotional energy can be quickly depleted.

Disappointments—which are inevitable—will be turned into discouragements unless within your heart there lies a silent, unseen, hidden pool of emotional power.

You'll need this reserve, for if your high hopes run out of heart-power to fuel enthusiasm and optimism, depression will take over. Pessimism will quickly clog the lines. Enthusiasm will wane. Energy will go. Power will be lost. Frustration and fatigue will drain the emotional tank dry. And burnout will end your trip!

What a tragedy for a plane to crash just after takeoff because the fuel tanks were empty!

Let me help you here. My life has been goal-dominated. The pressures and problems I've had to face have imposed incredible strain on my hopes and my heart. But I've never run out of emotional energy. The secret? My head has constantly been refueled with a power-generating faith in God, which is drawn from the depths of my heart.

202

As a person thinks in his heart, so is he. (PROVERBS 23:7)

Deep down in every heart there comes the call to believe in something divine, whether we call that something the Higher Power, the Supreme Intelligence, the Ultimate Spiritual Force in the universe—or God. As we come to the end of the twentieth century, we're seeing an amazing shift in the scientific perception of positive religion. DNA researchers are amazed at the incredible, intricate universe that's unfolding. The awesome engineering in the whole system boggles the mind. "There's a Transcendent Designer behind it all!" I'm told by pioneers in the exploration of genetic architecture.

Scientists are now talking about something they call the Anthropic Principle, which says (according to *Webster's Collegiate Dictionary*) that "the universe must have properties that make inevitable the existence of intelligent life." In other words, scientists are observing elements in the universe that are amazingly balanced to make human life possible.

We're approaching a new era, I predict. In that era atheism will be marked as a sign of scientific illiteracy. Something intelligent is "out there," out of sight; that's the new paradigm impacting physicists, chemists, and genetic researchers.

Connect with this cosmic Higher Power. Listen to the call of your heart of hearts to become a believer in God. Your heart calls to your mind to listen to the spiritual impulses deep within yourself. Become a believer, and your heart will never allow your head to give up in frustration or failure.

Let me tell you a story about two persons. Both are very powerful and most distinctive in that power. They live in the same house but don't communicate. She's always admired and respected him, but he's drifted from her. He's developed an itinerant lifestyle: he comes and goes. Where? And when? He never tells her. She leaves him a note, but a reply never comes. Is her note lost in the tons of paperwork that litter his desk? Is he so overwhelmed that the note hasn't been read? She tries a telephone call, hoping to leave a message of some urgency. His cellular phone rings over and over, but it isn't answered. She hangs up in frustration. She has such an urgent, lifesaving message! Serious and irreversible consequences will result if things are allowed to run their dangerous course. Desperate, she tries again—another number that the unreached one sometimes answers. One, two, three times the phone rings. Her spirits lift when the phone clicks on pickup but plummet again when she hears, "Leave a message, please. I'm not able to come to the phone right now. I'll return your call when I'm able." The tape-recorded message means well but won't keep its promise, for good or not-good reasons—it doesn't matter which. The connection doesn't happen.

These two very powerful persons fail to connect. Who are they? They represent the two persons who live within every human being, destined to share the same house. He's the head; she's the heart. In some people they've never been close. In others they were close but have drifted apart, either suddenly or slowly. But if they don't communicate, they'll both eventually die.

The head has been educated. He's become intellectually elite—smart, critical, logical—and in the ego-boosting process he no longer listens to his humble heart.

Now the heart is calling out to the head. She's the emotional self calling out for her mate—the cognitive self.

If only they'd touched and connected and found a mutually respecting relationship—how exciting, satisfying, and delightfully fulfilling their life might have been!

They were meant to be what the most beautiful marriage always is: mutually complementary—never competitive. Mutually affirming and encouraging—never insulting by either silence or sentences spoken. Always mutually honoring each other—never demeaning by uninvited distance, which generates distractions. Mutually uplifting—never condescending.

Yes, this is a story of two persons meant to live a life of creative love together. They were meant to be helpmates. Yet somewhere, somehow, they drifted apart; the head left the heart behind. In his heady pride, he just plain left her behind—and lost her. She was distinctively different and gifted. She was designed and destined to be his truest, best, and most beautiful and beloved and intimate friend. Now they live unspeaking, disconnected in the same house—a house haunted by dreams turning into despair.

It's a very normal and understandable—though disquieting—story. The two persons were destined to live together, but they were predesigned for different roles. Because there are different rules for different roles, they began to follow different guidelines. For him the rule is logic; for her the rule is love. For him the rule is intellect; for her the rule is emotion. The head—the heart. No wonder they can so easily drift apart. And yet this mustn't be allowed to happen. They desperately need each other! Without passion, the practical project loses its life-renewing energy.

Now the heart calls out to the head:

Listen to me! Listen to me—I'm your heart. Why do you never dare to let me be free to become what I was born to become? Your passionate power. Why do you close the door to me when I laugh and cry? When I sing my songs of hopes and hurts? Why do you always want to control everything and everyone who touches you—even me!

I'm your heart. There are mysterious, warm, refreshing, and renewing moods that I want to share with you! Forceful, fortifying, friendly feelings live with me. Why do you shut me out of your power plays? Are you afraid that I'll embarrass you? Or are you perhaps afraid that I'll upstage you?

I could and would be your best friend.

Be honest with me. You don't need to be afraid to tell me if you're tired, bewildered, confused, or overwhelmed. I'm the one and only friend you can trust with your secret dreams and your sad hurts—and even your vain ambitions.

Come to me. Are you lost? I can see another way from where I live. The heart can see a path that's out of sight to the head—a path you'll surely overlook, left alone on your lofty perch up there, too distracted by your world to see the real world where I live. I live on the level of laughter, tears, and—yes—prayer.

Believe me, if you remain alone—nothing but mental muscles—you'll lose heart; and if you do, you'll give up and fail.

You must know that you need me. You're lost without the joy that I alone can give.

You're always so busy and in such a hurry that you never have time to sit alone with me.

When was the last time you "searched your heart"? You always have time for your "friends." You've made a lot of strong but strange and foreign acquaintances through the years, but will they prove to be your true friends at the end of the road?

Few (if any) of them know me. You've never introduced them to me. You listen to them without thinking what it means to me to be kept apart! Oh, my head—open a door to me!

I'm your heart!

Go now to the secret drawer where you keep the extra keys, that drawer you haven't touched for years. Inside is the key that will release the joyful tomorrows that only I can give you. It's the key to our private place, where only the two of us can go. Find it. Open the door. Turn and smile at me again. Call for me to come to you. Touch me. Invite me to join you alone. Here we'll listen to each other. We'll love each other. Laugh together. Cry together.

Yes, we need each other. What's power without comradeship? What's success without spiritual fulfillment? What's a head without a heart?

I have words you need to hear. I have music to lift you from your loneliness. Listen to me, my best one, my bright and wise one. For too long you've been controlled by the loud sounds and the sirens on the fast road where you run every day. The chaotic sounds confuse you.

You need the peaceful power that only I can give you. Do you hear a soft sound now? A distant voice? A far-off melody? What is it? What have you been missing? Who's out there—crowded out, pushed away in the wild scene where you've been living? It's I—the silent spirit you haven't felt.

It's I. I'm calling your name. I'm your best friend. I'm your heart calling out for you to welcome me back to your side, to fill your emptiness with the private power of my passionate presence.

Come! Let's sing together a new song. Here are the happy words by Santayana:

> Oh world, thou chooseth not the better part.
> It is not wisdom to be only wise
> and on the inward vision close the eyes
> But it is wisdom to believe the heart.
> Columbus found a world and had no chart.
> Save one that faith deciphered in the skies.
> To trust the soul's invincible surmise
> was all his science and his only art.
> Our knowledge is a torch of smokey pine
> that lights the pathway, but one step ahead

across a void of mystery and dread.
Bid then the tender light of faith to shine
by which alone the mortal heart is led
into the thinking of the Thought Divine.

Listen to me, my honored one, for God lives within your heart. Come to me. Sense the Holy Spirit that fills this heart of yours. Connect with me and come to love and listen to the God within you.

Yes, I'm connected to the Eternal Love—that Being who promised, "I will never leave you or forsake you" (Deuteronomy 31:6). Welcome this Living Spirit into your thinking, and you'll never, never, never fail!

Connect with the God who lives in your heart. Fill your possibility-thinking brain with heart-power—with what I might call faith!

Will you—my reader friend—have the emotional energy that your goals demand from you? Yes—if you're connected to the eternal God who gave you the power of intuition along with the gift of intelligence.

The price must be paid. Connect with the God who gave you a head and a heart.

You're now in a holy and humble partnership with the Higher Power that mixed the genes into the one-of-a-kind person called you. Two priceless, precious gifts are yours: life and God's dream to be and become a bright light in a dark world.

Now trust Him; He'll speak to you from your heart of hearts, renewing you so that you'll never lack the emotional energy to keep on keeping on. He's promised again and again and again, "I will never leave you or forsake you."

He also says, "When you go through the waters they will not overflow you. When you go through the fire it will not consume you. For I know your name. I have redeemed you. I will be with you" (Isaiah 43:1 and 2).

And you'll hear this promise from Saint Paul: "If God is for you, who can be against you?" (Romans 8:31).

Price 2

MANAGE YOUR TIME PRODUCTIVELY

You say you're prepared to pay the emotional price? Now prepare yourself to pay the price in time. Time management is the next key that you'll need to unlock the door to eventual success. You'll need to set and establish a timeframe for your dream.

Never reject and abandon your God-inspired dream by declaring, "I don't have the time." You don't, perhaps—but God does. So let go and let God! Your schedule will need to be reorganized to make the time to turn new mountains into marvelous miracles.

Do a fresh, up-to-the-minute review of your priorities. Go back and reread the chapter titled "Priorities Must Be Swayed." You and you alone will decide what projects, plans, and persons must be reprioritized to make time today to do what must be done sooner, not later.

How do I find the time to manage a weekly worldwide television ministry? And write books? And build a strong and happy family based on a loving marriage that's close to a joyous fiftieth anniversary?

I learned early in life how and when to "retire." I've now passed the forty-year anniversary in my ministerial work. At the end of my first year on the job as pastor I began to "retire." I retired from the job of janitor, for example. I haven't cleaned floors or toilets since! And that retirement freed up time for other duties. At the end of my second year I retired from my job as secretary, no longer typing my own letters. I found time to do other worthwhile church work. At the end of my third year I retired as business manager. I haven't deposited money or written a check for the parish since then. I was released to use my time more productively. At the end of my fourth year I retired as department leader and teacher. I found the church a better replacement, and I had more time to write. At the end of my fifth year, then sixth year—yes, every passing year—I retired from further time-consuming duties. At the end of my tenth year I finally retired as marriage counselor. The Counseling Center was opened and staffed as part of our ministry, and I found a lot of time—time that was instantly filled with new ideas that needed top priority on my clock and calendar. At the end of my fifteenth year we launched the television ministry, and I retired as the senior minister managing the staff of the large local congregation. At the end of my twenty-fifth year I retired as my car driver. I can now read books, dictate letters, and read my mail—all from the back seat of a car. At the end of my fortieth year I retired from five days a week in the office to become a minister at large in the world, filling a role only my face and name could fill.

Learn how to retire selectively from those duties you've always done. Focus on the role where you're irreplaceable. You'll be surprised at how well, wisely, and fruitfully your time will then be managed.

Yes, you can find time if you learn how, and when, and from what you must retire. It's easy to say goodbye if you have a higher, holier invitation to a new hello!

Lord,
help me to know
when to say
goodbye
and
when to say
hello,
And give me the wisdom
to make the
transition with
grace, courage, and kindness.
Amen

Make the time to allow bigger, better, and more beautiful things to happen.

Only you can do that. "If it's going to be, it's up to me."

Time is the one thing that can't be replaced.

Manage your time, and you'll manage to succeed in accomplishing what appear to be impossible goals.

Nothing is impossible! Some things just take a long—or longer!—time.

Nothing is impossible! I just have to learn when and what to delegate to whom.

Nothing is impossible! I just have to make better use of my hours and years.

What goals could you achieve if you blocked out ten years? Fifteen years? Twenty years? Thirty years? Forty years? Move your thinking from a clock to a calendar. Then nothing is impossible!

"But I'm too old. I don't have the years left," you say.

You may live longer than you or anyone else imagines. *People* magazine in their January 15, 1996 issue tells the story of Jeanne Calment, a French woman who lives in an apartment that sits over what used to be her late husband's fab-

216

ric shop. There young Jeanne sold canvas to Vincent van Gogh. When Andre-François Raffray agreed to buy Jeanne Calment's four-room apartment in Arles, France, in 1965, he thought he was getting a good deal. Under the French *vigor* (or "for life") system, Raffray, a notary public, would pay Calment the equivalent of five hundred dollars a month and allow her to live in the flat until her death. In return, he would own the apartment when she died and could have room to expand his adjacent office. Such arrangements are common enough in France, and since Calment was ninety years old, how long could she last? Last year Raffray went to his grave still wondering.

Raffray, seventy-seven, died of cancer at his home in Arles on Christmas Day, having paid Calment more than a hundred and seventy-five thousand dollars—about three times the value of the apartment. Calment, meanwhile, at one hundred and twenty (and the oldest documented person alive), dined on salad with chicken liver, roast duck, and *bûche de Noël* as the guest star at a banquet hosted by the mayor of Arles. Although she wasn't told of Raffray's passing, she would likely have been sympathetic. "It happens in life that we make bad deals," she teased Raffray on her birthday the previous February.

Go on!

don't

Go under!

and you'll

Go over!

With Raffray's death, his son and daughter will be required to continue the monthly payment to Calment. And they might take note of her unflagging joie de vivre. Asked recently how she'd feel about living to age one hundred and twenty-five, her response was simple: "Why be pessimistic?"

My wife's mother was born in 1900. She's had several major life-threatening challenges. Today, as I write these words, she's celebrating her ninety-sixth birthday. Her goals? To become the best piano and organ player in the peaceful and really pleasant rest home where she lives. How alive she is!

And Dr. Armand Hammer was in his nineties when he formulated a new goal—to bring religion to the USSR. The year was 1989. The Cold War was still on. That success is now history!

Be smart. Just think: if you live to be one hundred, like George Burns, and if you're eighty today—you could come up with a new twenty-year goal!

I'm seventy years old as I write these words. My mission statement reads, "Build a positive church that will impact the world for the next few hundred years as St. Peter's in Rome has done for the past half-millennium." In support of this mission statement, I have a new goal intended to keep the power base from cracking and crumbling through unpredictable downturns in the decades and centuries to come. Is such a goal possible? Yes, if I'm willing to pay the price in time. All I have to do is think longer, think smarter, and think bigger!

Again and again as I study people we might describe as failures, I see dreamers who just couldn't think big or bravely enough to pay the price that their dreams were demanding in the currency of time. Wise time management could have turned their impossibilities into possibilities, and it will do the same for you. The smartest purchase you'll ever make might be the price you pay in time.

Price 3

DEALING WITH THE DOLLAR COSTS

Your goals? My goals? They're achievable if we're willing to pay the price in emotions and time. But we have to be prepared to pay the monetary price as well. And while it doesn't cost a dime to dream, acting on our dreams can be pretty pricey. Prohibitively so? Never!

If your heart is running with your head . . .

If you manage your time effectively . . .

Then money needs can and will be met someway, someday.

There are financial demands associated with almost any goal you might set. So yes, there's that price to be paid too. But no one ever needs to fail because of it. There's so much money on the move all the time; there are so many people looking for opportunities in which to invest. If the primary principles of achievement are clearly understood and faithfully applied at every level in the process of success, then any so-called money problems can be managed successfully.

What have I learned from personal experience about facing the mountain called "financial challenge"? Let me share some of what I've discovered as we've progressed from our start-up forty years ago—five hundred dollars in the bank and a drive-in theater for a church—to what we have today. The church property is now a debt-free development of "art in architecture." It's an investment worth well over one hundred million dollars—again, debt-free. The income that first year was twelve thousand dollars, which covered everything. The budget today is over a million dollars a week.

The monetary price certainly must be paid; experience has taught me that. Here's what else I've learned.

1. **The dollar price isn't the first, foremost challenge.** As I said, it doesn't cost a dime to dream. And every dream has a magnetic power that can attract money from the shadows. The inherent value of the dream and the integrity and credibility of the dreamer, when added together, generate the financial gravitational pull of the imagined project.

So the cost of the dream is the last issue to be addressed. Never did or do we allow our ministry's board of directors to respond to a new dream by asking, "What will it cost?" Initially only questions testing the dream's validity and value are allowed. What good will the project do? Who needs the service? Are we in the right position to move in the proposed direction? Does this expansion clearly fit our mission statement? The answers to questions such as these tell us how to face the financial challenge.

2. **The second thing I've learned is this: good ideas promoted by good people will al-**

ways get the attention of people with money. There's a vast pool of money out there just waiting to make a move!

3. **People with money are always looking for persons, projects, or places backed by purpose and plans, in which to invest.** They may either donate (assuming the cause is charitable) or invest money if the cause is potentially profitable.

4. **Start small; think tall; invest your all; send out a call!** If trustworthy people with great ideas do these things, money will flow toward them. One of the world's richest corporations, based in Korea, was founded by a friend of mine who had nothing initially. When I visited the country at the end of the Korean War on an Air Force assignment, he was collecting cigarette butts at the air base and selling the "used" tobacco. That's how he raised and saved his first hundred dollars! Once safely in the bank, that money increased to one thousand dollars. He started small. And where did he end up? His operation did seventy-five billion dollars' worth of business worldwide in the year 1996.

Start small; think tall—and invest your all in your dream! Pay the price and it will return, I've learned.

None are so poor

that they have

nothing to give . . .

and None are

so rich that they

have nothing

to receive.

—Pope John Paul II

5. **"Getting" always comes to the "giving" person.** I believe very firmly that this principle is primary, paramount, and nonnegotiable. The Holy Bible teaches that any money—or crop from a field—that comes to us must be "tithed." In accordance with that teaching, I've always given back to God ten percent of any money that's come to me.

I was taught this in my young years: "Every dollar you ever get: give ten percent to God, save another ten percent and invest it wisely, and live on the balance." If you can't live on eighty cents out of every dollar earned, then you're living too high! Scale down your living standard—or earn more money. You can! Trust God. Give Him His share first, and He'll more than repay you. My testimony is that God is a very generous God!

John Crean started his business in his garage. His first dollars earned—and they were meager indeed—were tithed. He never failed. Today he gives not ten percent but fifty percent of his income back to God and the community. His tithe launched the Crystal Cathedral with a million-dollar gift. As I write these lines, the business pages report that he's just gotten another sixty million dollars in income this year through a stock sale!

The price must be paid! And that includes giving God His thank-you!

6. The most important lesson I've learned about paying the price is one I've already shared with you: **No person, no project, and no institution ever faces a "money problem"; it's always an "idea problem" or an "attitude problem."**

I'm often asked to share success principles in seminars for top CEOs. I write this sentence on a board: "If there's a market for your product or your services but you're not making it, first check manufacturing, then check merchandising, then check marketing, and if you still aren't making it, it must be in management."

Manufacturing. Are you really building a better mousetrap? There will always be competition. If there's none, there soon will be. Your success will inspire competitors to choose a percentage of the market that you've proven is possible and profitable. Thus a commitment to excellence must be systemic in your possibility thinking. Even the best that's on the market won't last long. Smart (and even smarter) people are driven by the compulsion to improve whatever's working and winning in the free market, which is constantly appraising the latest and best options and alternatives.

Leadership is always on the edge of thinking about improving what the company or organization is doing. "Preventive management" can recognize and positively handle all challenges—real today or on the horizon. It can meet those challenges before they become genuine obstacles and negatively impact the organization's mission, demanding "crisis management."

Change is constantly buffeting us in "systems" that affect our life and work. Think about the changes in design and delivery that must be confronted regularly by those in business—and not with a cavalier attitude but rather with a creative mental appraisal. New inventions are always coming on line. Even if the inventions you know about are in industries that don't obviously relate to your chosen enterprise, could they be adaptable in an innovative move to improve or enhance your own product or service? Think about the drive-in concept. First used by hamburger outlets, it was soon adopted by banks, then theaters, then churches. Computers? Ask yourself where this technology hasn't yet been applied. I'm tired of all of the keys I have to carry; the collection is cumbersome and confusing. I'm waiting for a small, light computer chip that can be programmed to unlock any door I need to open, start any motor, and/or ignite any electrical connection. Someone will make it happen someday, and that development will make an enormous impact on manufacturing.

Money problems? Really? Then first check manufacturing. Excellence has great power to attract new financial support. Money is like water: it will flow to newer and better ideas.

Merchandising. Perhaps your so-called money problems are really merchandising problems instead. What do I mean by merchandising? How your product, person, invention, or concept is presented. Is it attractive? Can you improve on the packaging of your product or service to make it more appealing to your clients, consumers, or customers?

Beauty is practical too. Style may be as important as substance to help you promote your product or service. Once you've checked your manufacturing (and improved your product or service accordingly), can you then improve your packaging, presentation, or promotion?

Can the box be a see-through package? Can the sales presentation be "packaged" in a personality that's emotionally "well dressed" and that radiates enthusiasm from a friendly, smiling face?

Marketing. Money problems? Think again.

Take a closer look at your enterprise. If you've already taken the first steps—you know there's a market for your product or service, and you've determined that your merchandising is effective—then check marketing.

Now stop right there. Double-check the market if you're still not making it. Has it started slowly dying? And ask yourself whether your product or service is "fashionable" or "classical"?

If it's fashionable—a fad, in other words—get smart and get out. As suspected, you don't have a money problem; you have an idea problem.

If it's classical, find a smarter marketing plan and stick with your product or service. Look for effective ways to get the word out. In the marketing of books, publishers target the top TV talkshows, hoping that their authors can appear to "expose" (and thereby sell) their new books. The best shot? The morning network shows. *Good Morning America,* for example. *The Today Show.* "You'll sell four thousand copies in the bookstores of America if you get on a top network morning show," I was told. And it was true: I had that experience more than once.

In the marketing of my latest book I was

asked to appear on QVC. I was told that on one day I would make three eighteen-minute appearances on this home-shopping television network and that we would sell fifteen thousand copies if they were personally autographed. I couldn't believe it! But I agreed. I stepped into a huge building that housed live television studios, one of which had on hand fifteen thousand autographed copies of my book. (Yes, all fifteen thousand copies were personally autographed by me.)

"We'll sell them all today!" the station representatives promised. "You'll be seen and heard by millions of people watching us via the television cables across America. All they have to do is pick up the telephone and call in their order. We have thousands of computerized telephone answering services right here! Just look at our computer screen."

I couldn't believe it! Use the latest marketing system to sell a single inspirational book? In a matter of minutes three thousand lines had lighted up! At the end of my third appearance only a few hours later, all fifteen thousand copies were sold!

Marketing! Perhaps the new marketing in your field involves direct mail, catalogue sales, retailing through a major chain of stores, an "infomercial," or a sidewalk sale. Be creative. Be innovative. Find an imaginative new way to deliver your product or service to the people who need it—but who don't know that they need it or that you have it for them.

I deliver what started out as the first nationally televised church service in America—providing emotional food to people who've never gone to church. Through innovative TV "marketing," I offer my "product," which is spiritual food that offers healthy, lifesaving nourishment.

Money problems? How do we—on television—collect an offering or receive donations? No church of any faith can succeed without public contributions. Enter direct mail. Pass the offering plate through the mailbox. Dignified? Absolutely! People who choose not to give don't have to feel embarrassed because they let the offering plate pass without dropping anything in. They simply throw my letter in the wastebasket. But if we offer a service that has integrity and that delivers hope and help to feed and nourish positive thinking, then enough listeners will respond to keep our spiritual "business" alive. And so for twenty-seven years we've succeeded; in fact, at this writing we're the longest-running and most widely viewed television church service in the world.

Now, a quick review. If there's an authentic market for your product or service and you're not making it, first check manufacturing, then check merchandising, then check marketing; and if all three areas check out and you're still not making it, the problem has to be in . . .

Management. You don't have a money problem; you have a management problem.

Waste? Check it out! Bravely, carefully. The winner's edge between success and failure is often very thin. Why do some enterprises survive when so many fail? Largely because they courageously and cautiously avoid wasting money, or spending it unwisely.

"Can we deliver the product better and cheaper?" This is a question you must frequently ask. It's not easy to cut costs. Determining how you can do so is never painless. It's responsible management, though. Remember my earlier definition of management? It's the control of expenditures to maximize top-quality productivity at the lowest possible cost.

Good management is a challenge! One of its primary responsibilities is to identify the idea problem or attitude problem behind the apparent money problem.

Because of a tornado my family lost everything when I was in college. Where would the tuition money come from now? I had no scholarship. I knew no rich people. I'd have to find a job to earn money while carrying a full load of classes. But jobs were really scarce during those years. Then I discovered that there were always some jobs even during times of great unemployment. I took a job as a janitor, sweeping floors and cleaning toilets during my "off" hours. I didn't have a money problem; I just needed to work on my attitude! I paid the price—with my heart, my time, and the careful expenditure of hard-earned dollars.

I learned the lesson well: my dream would come true if I was willing to pay the price and if I never, never, never gave up!

I learned . . .

If it's going to be, it's up to me!

What have you learned thus far from this book? You've learned lessons in personal responsibility.

Over twenty years ago a young salesman listened to my primary lessons in possibility thinking. He heard. He understood. He paid the price. Today he's moved from the threat of poverty into the world of prosperity. He's one of the strongest and best-loved members of my church, as well as an extremely successful lecturer and author. Listen to what he's learned:

Declaration of Personal Responsibility

by Danny Cox

I currently possess everything I have truly wanted and deserved. My possessions, my savings, and my lifestyle are an exact mirror of me, my efforts, and my contribution to society. What I give, I get. If I am unhappy with what I have received, it is because, as yet, I have not paid the required price. I have lingered too long in the "quibbling stage."

I fully understand that time becomes a burden to me only when it is empty. The past is mine, and at this very moment I am purchasing another twenty-four hours of it. The future transitions quickly into the past at a control point called the present moment. I not only truly live at that point, but have full responsibility for the highest and best use of the irreplaceable now.

I accept full responsibility for both the

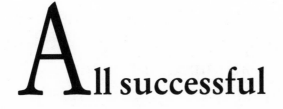

All successful people are experienced in failure.

successes and failures in my life. If I am not what I desire to be at this point, what I am is my compromise. I choose no longer to compromise with my undeveloped potential.

I am the sum total of the choices I have made and continue to choose daily. What I now put under close scrutiny is the value of each upcoming choice. Therein lies the quality of my future lifestyle.

Will my future belong to the "old me" or the "new me"? The answer depends on my attitude toward personal growth at this very moment. What time is left is all that counts, and that remaining time is my responsibility. With a newfound maturity I accept full responsibility for how good I can become at what is most important to me.

With personal growth comes a fear of the unknown and new problems. Those problems are nothing more than the increasing shadow of my personal growth. I now turn my very real fear, with God's help, into a very real adventure.

My life now expands to meet my newfound destiny. "Old me," meet the "new me."

People who hear me talk about the dollar costs

of pursuing one's dream often ask me, "What about the poor? Will they—the have-nots of this world—be able to pay the price their dream demands? Does this book work only for the privileged, the affluent?"

Will this rugged individualism work for the poor? Well, yes and no.

No, if the poor are unemployable. That includes the severely handicapped and the very old. Certainly there are persons so handicapped by mental or physical ill-health that they can't make it without generous help from caregiving achievers and a caring, compassionate society.

But rugged individualism works for the vast majority of the poor who dare to try to succeed. The economist James Glassman reported, "New research looked at Americans who were in the bottom quintile [that's the lowest fifth of income earners] in 1979 and the groups were checked out again in 1991. Only 5% were still at the bottom, while 59% had moved to the top or the next to the top quintile."

Yes, the principles of success in this book work to fight poverty the honorable, dignified way—at least in the United States of America. The poor don't stay poor for long when they learn responsible lessons of success in possibility thinking.

So go for it! Life is easy only when you're going downhill!

Come alive! Stop floating and start swimming. As the old saying goes, even a dead fish can float downstream.

Afraid? Well, even a turtle can't get ahead without sticking its neck out.

Be brave. Courage isn't feeling free from fear; courage is facing the fears you feel.

VI

THE TIMING
MAY BE DELAYED

N ow it's time to practice hanging tough. That's a necessity, because every accomplishment, every success, has to go through tough times. After a quarter-century of specializing in human motivation, I came to a crystal-clear conclusion—one that became the title of a book: *Tough Times Never Last, But Tough People Do.*

Possibility thinkers succeed in large part because they're sensitive to timing. Their sense of timing is astonishing. Their courage to be positively impulsive is impressive.

Timing is everything!

These classic lines have been in my mind all my life:

Be not the first to lay the old aside.
Nor yet the last by which the new is tried.

But I haven't always followed that counsel. Again and again my divine direction has called me to be a "point man." In military strategy the point man is the first person to lead his troops into unexplored territory. Sometimes success demands that of us. But there's no simple formula: many people with great new ideas have failed because they were "ahead of their time," while many other great achievers have succeeded because they were patient in moving ahead.

Leaders know that timing is crucial, critical. There's no arbitrary advice I can give here, except this: develop a strong sense of timing. I credit God for the successful timing in my life. I couldn't have made it without prayer.

What's really awesome is the possibility thinker's power to deal with unexpected delays. Patience is the possibility thinker's all-powerful secret weapon.

The timing may be delayed. That's bad news!

But wait a minute! Just think: bad news can always be turned by possibility thinkers into good news.

Yes, true—and not a few failures happen when a move is made too fast.

I sense that the greatest mistake made in timing is impatience. The lesson of patience must be learned loud and clear, again and again, in the process of success.

Check your history. See how the heroic characters have made it with purpose, passion, and patience. Remember Mahatma Gandhi and Martin Luther King, Jr. Think about Nelson Mandela: he lived twenty-three years in an island prison before apartheid finally fell and he was released to become the first president of an integrated South Africa. And consider the scientists who've reached the age of nearly eighty—or beyond!—before their life's work has been recognized and rewarded with the highest honor: the Nobel Prize. Likewise, check out the Nobel Peace Prize winners.

Again and again the success of important and heroic figures such as these has been made possible because of their toughness, their ability to hang on through tough years—yes, decades—with unbending, unyielding commitment to their cause.

I once studied the lives of persons and families that had risen from a low economic level to financial independence, their financial base delivering an annual dividend to cover all their financial needs even through their hard times. How did they make it? Not by the lottery. Again and again, they earned a little, saved a little, and spent less—and waited while they watched their investment grow. Patience is power!

—∞—

Passion + Timing = Success

—∞—

I've heard that equation hundreds of times from my friends in the American Academy of Achievement. Every year this distinguished academy meets to welcome new honorees. Its members include:

- Nobel Prize winners in the sciences, arts, and humanities
- Pulitzer Prize winners in literature
- Oscar winners in the cinematic arts
- Political and corporate leaders—all world-class achievers
- Athletes and artists

Great achievers—you'll meet them here. And almost every one of them will agree with our equation: Passion + Timing = Success.

Time out! How many persons are victims of

Every

achievement

is a process,

not an

instamatic

happening.

our Instamatic mentality? The Polaroid Instamatic camera has become a symbol of a radical cultural change. "I want it now" acts as a subconscious, subtle enemy to many would-be entrepreneurs. These people set goals. Good. They mark their calendars. Good again. But unrealistic expectations in timing are a danger they fail to recognize. With their Instamatic mind-set, they don't allow enough time for the phases, the steps, the stages, and the levels of their dreams to be processed.

The timing may be delayed? For you and your dream? Well, what did you expect? Internal and external conflict is almost always the result of unfulfilled expectations, often on the deeper level of nonverbalized, ambiguous presumptions and anticipations. Clarify and specify your expectations.

Were you expecting too much too soon? Almost always—in virtually every positive process—achievement takes longer than you planned. Impatient entrepreneurs simply get depressed, angry, or frustrated—and then quit.

The all-important lesson of this chapter is this: Become a master of time management. Timing is everything!

Opportunities are all around you. And often they come without advance notice; but almost always they come with a great possibility in their right hand and a clock and a calendar in their left hand.

I repeat, timing is everything. The greatest defenders of freedom have been the leaders in the military. "Is the time right?" they ask. "Are we prepared for the attack? Should we wait until our weak areas are made strong? Or must we move now?"

Yes, timing is everything. Often success, survival, and even freedom demand that you move. Tonight! Now! Fast! Leave everything behind and make a run for it. The door is open now. Wait, and it will be locked, perhaps forever.

General John M. Shalikashvili holds the highest military position in the United States of America: chairman of the joint chiefs of staff. He shared at a recent gathering of the American Academy of Achievement what his family (who lived then in Poland) had done when the Soviet army moved in. "We had to move now! Immediately! . . . We left everything and escaped to Berlin. I was six years old. We dreamed of making it to America. Now it was time to wait. I was nine years old when we arrived in Peoria, Illinois.

"I travel a great deal in and out of my adopted country, and never, never do I ever come back to this country without profound love for America. It's a miracle every time I re-enter my homeland."

My eyes locked with the general's. Deep into his soul I probed, and there I saw faith! "You have a strong faith?" I asked him privately.

"Yes," he said, immediately opening up. "I'm Orthodox." The head of the Orthodox Church is Jesus Christ.

"Now I know where your power comes from," I said. I'd sensed and seen power in him, and now I understood. When believers use the word God, they refer to that awesome Guiding Force—the God who can motivate us, either fast or slow.

Yes, timing is everything! When a sudden opportunity comes and the window is open, neither nature nor God will wait. This realization brings with it a command: Look. Listen. Today. Now! Prepare to move! Get ready to go when the bell rings. First one out will win. Be alert. Competition is keen. On your toes!

Once out, watch your timing! Pace yourself. Do you think you should start fast and get the lead position? Or would it be better to start a bit slower and reserve your full and fastest output of limited energy for the last lap?

Athletes know that timing is everything.

Professional fund-raisers know this too. They know that fund-raising always follows friend-raising. Too hurried in your solicitation and you'll "flush the bird." Too slow and you'll miss your chance. An example:

A dear and close friend of mine called to tell me that he wanted to leave a four-thousand-acre ranch to our church in his will. "Have your staff person come to see me," he said, "and I'll sign the papers. I'm going into the hospital for a little surgery. He can come and see me there."

That was a Monday. The staff person waited too long. When he called on Friday, it was already too late. Only two hours before, my friend the benefactor had died—without a chance to alter his will as he desired.

Will you know if you must be swift—or patient? If God is your God, I think you'll see, sense, and seize the moment. The swift unwaiting opportunities are often very clear and clean in their surprising appearance. Intuitively you know you've been confronted with a possibility. Impetuously, impulsively, impertinently, you have to shift your priorities. You make your move. You look back later, astonished! You scored a great success, for your timing was right on.

Perhaps a job opened up and you were there. Being "the right person at the right spot at the right time"—that says it all. Think of the unknown actress who "happened" to be at the right place at the right time. She met a screenwriter who said, "Read this." She did, and she liked it, though no one else wanted the part. She took it and did well. As it turns out, the market was ready for this kind of a movie: it was nominated for an Oscar! Yes!

God is involved in our timing. Of that I'm sure. I didn't choose the century into which I would be born, but I was certainly the right person in the right place at the right time.

Spontaneity—it's a powerful gift. Sense it. Study it. Be available to it. Be alert, active, and aggressive, so that you can swiftly respond to the powerful potential of an unexpected opportunity that won't wait.

"Positively impulsive" describes so many of the achievers I know. "Make it happen now" are four words that have motivated many a superstar.

And positive impulsivity works for the positively reactive person as well as the proactive person. When Woolworth opened his store, his competitor ran a huge ad that read, "We've been in business fifty years." Woolworth, with an unknown name, grabbed the moment. A rapid response was needed. Now—or he'd be dead! Spontaneity to the rescue. He ran an ad that he hadn't planned on running: "We've been in business only one week, and all the merchandise on all our shelves is really new!" The rest is history!

And Woolworth stores are still supersuccessful.

Because good timing is everything, let's devote some time to three skills that can help you fine-tune your timing.

<u>Skill 1</u>

RECOGNIZE THAT TIMING IS ALL-IMPORTANT IN ALL OF LIFE

Whoever we talk to, whatever we see—everything around us is dependent on good timing.

In **nature**, timing is nonnegotiable. Seasons come and go on their own uncompromising schedule. From seed to flower, timing is predetermined.

The **business world** also bows to timing. Timing isn't democratic. Seasons set the marketing agenda. "When should we start selling Christmas items?" In December? After Thanksgiving? In September? "When should we discount spring clothes?" While it's still late spring?

Entertainers sharpen their sensitivity to— and skill in—timing. Effective communicators in all fields learn the art of using pauses in their delivery to give the audience time to catch up.

Lovers are in tune with timing. The first touch. Then the flow of trust. Then the first embrace. A good sense of timing tells them when to move and when to hold back.

Psychologists and **consultants in relationships** intuitively take timing into account. Listen to the questions they ask their clients: "How old . . . ?" "How long . . . ?" "When did you first . . . ?" "How often do you . . . ?"

Health-care specialists listen to the body's call for time to heal, to restore, to build power into bones and muscles and nerves. "We'll just have to wait and give the heart and body time to respond to therapy or treatment."

Economists are quick to see the power of time in allowing assets to earn dividends that, if left to accumulate interest year after year, turn a modest initial investment into a major growth account.

Addiction recovery therapists see the timing factor as all-important. Drinking too much? Addicted to bad eating habits? "He's going to have to hit a low before he'll actually be responsive. Let's wait a bit."

Scriptwriters must be gifted at timing too. Emotional peaks must be staged and paced to build momentum and hold interest. And almost every movie exploits timing by "cutting to the chase."

Career managers are onto the timing factor as well. "Is she ready to make a career change?" "Does he need to take time to learn computer skills?" "Is the timing right for her to move on?"

Success consultants know that timing is everything. "Is he the right person with the right skills in the right spot at the right time?"

Entrepreneurs also know that timing is everything. More than one person has failed because he was "ahead of his time." People are often offered this wise advice: "You need to spend more time in preparation and training; you're not ready yet." Other people have failed because they moved too cautiously, too slowly. Analysts might correctly conclude, "They were too late getting in the market." Or "By the time they made their move, the field was already overloaded."

Skill 2

DISCIPLINE YOURSELF WITH THE POSITIVE MENTAL ATTITUDE OF PATIENCE

Anyone who lacks the ability to deal with delay after delay will fail, fall apart, and come unhinged in this imperfect, complex world. That's why you need to discipline yourself with the positive mental attitude of patience.

Our maintenance people have a long-standing order never to delay in replacing a broken window. Usually that order is promptly followed. So when a window broke and days—and then weeks—passed and it still wasn't repaired, I was upset. Then I received this memo from the staff person in charge:

> I want to give you a rundown on the events that occurred recently.
>
> As you know, on June 22 one of the windows was broken. I contacted our vendor to board up the opening. On June 25 they came out and measured. They contacted a glass manufacturer in Florida for a price. I gave them the okay to order; however, when they called to place the order on June 27, the manufacturer informed them that they were in the process

of moving and would not be operational for six weeks instead of the original three weeks.

On June 28 they contacted a manufacturer in Oregon who could deliver in three weeks. On July 1 they requoted the glass to me and I gave them the okay for ordering. They closed for July 4 and 5. On July 8 the order was placed with the company. On July 11 they called to say they were having trouble finding the oversized glass. On July 15 they found the glass in Washington State for a hundred dollars more. I gave them the okay. On July 17 and 18, in the process of firing the panes, they broke two. On July 29 the shipper totaled his truck, and they had to find a new truck and driver.

On August 6 we finally got word that the glass was en route. It arrived at the local shop on August 8. When they went to load it on the truck for transporting it the next morning, it shattered into a million pieces. We then had to reorder the glass on August 9. On August 27 the new glass arrived at the local shop. When they went to put it on the truck on August 28, their truck had a flat tire.

They quickly fixed this, and I'm happy to report that the new glass was put in Wednesday without incident.

Delays and more delays! Patience—we needed it!

Skill 3

PUT A POSITIVE SPIN ON DELAYS

You've got your short-range, intermediate-range, and long-range goals marked on your calendar. When you fall short on the time you allotted for a particular level of achievement, what do you do? Quit? Of course not. You try to put a positive spin on the time crunch. Grab hold of this chapter title and see it as a positive encouragement: your timing may have to be delayed. Possibility thinkers do this all the time. I could share a truckload of true stories on this subject with you. For instance:

- **College students who couldn't make it in the prescribed four years.** In six or eight or ten years, those students proudly accepted their diplomas, and today they're very successful in their careers.
- **Homeowners who were saving money**

for a down payment only to be caught by a sudden interest-rate increase and a tight mortgage before they had the needed funds. Quit? Of course not. They simply said, "The timing needs to be delayed"—and they saved some more. Five or even ten years later—after waiting for their savings to grow, for the seller's market to slow, and for interest rates to drop—they were finally able to make that down payment and move in.

Putting a positive spin on delays is such an essential element of success that it deserves a bit more attention. Let's look at some of the benefits a delay can offer:

1. **A delay offers the chance to make some really good changes.** In the rush of hurrying to meet deadlines, you've probably put a lot of other things on the back burner. A delay gives you time to . . .

- Revise your plans
- Revitalize and rest
- Rebuild relationships
- Reorganize or restructure
- Refinance

2. **A delay gives you the chance to improve quality.** A delay could mean you'd move your achievement from mediocrity to excellence. Achievers are committed to accomplishment with excellence.

An old story from India proves this point. A teacher poured milk into a glass until it was full to the top.

"Is there room for more?" the teacher asked.

All the students shook their heads: "No more room."

Then the teacher slipped a gold ring from his finger, dropped it into the pitcher, and said, "There's always room for more quality."

3. **A delay presents the opportunity to work longer and smarter.**

One of the twentieth century's most famous lawyers was the late Louis Nizer, a good friend. "What are the most motivational words you've encountered in your career?" I asked him one night at a private dinner.

"That's easy," he answered. "Every year when I'm invited by the Yale University Law School to lecture to the new students, I give them these lines I wrote years ago":

"There is one wonderful word
I want to leave with you.

It makes the stupid person bright.
It makes the bright person brilliant.
It makes the brilliant person steady.
It is a mystic word.
It opens any and all portals.
It is work!"

Louis Nizer smiled. "And then, Dr. Schuller, I tell them, 'All cases are won by thorough preparation.'"

There we have it: how to make our mark. Work! That's how we can initiate the evolutionary development of noble achievement.

Possibility thinking isn't just dreaming. It's faith in action. That translates into W-O-R-K with a patient commitment to excellence.

Check out the achievers: students, athletes, salespersons, educators, bankers, entrepreneurs, scientists, businesspersons, professional career persons (in medicine, law, the ministry). All achievers are achievers because they love to work!

Work. W-O-R-K. Connect this concept to the knowledge that timing is everything, and you realize that at every level, and at every stage in the process of pressing to achieve your goals, you must work—harder, longer, and smarter.

Yes, you need to have patience, but that's

no excuse to lie back lazily. Exerting patience means using more time to improve the quality of your work.

4. **A delay can increase your good reputation.** If you delay in order to have a better product or service, you'll come to be known as a person who really wants to be helpful, honest, and trustworthy.

A Horatio Alger brother of mine started business with a single gasoline station. "How can I make it with all the other gas stations around here?" he wondered. What more could he offer to attract customers? His competition offered everything he offered in terms of product, hours of opening, and great service.

"May I check your oil?" he always asked.

One customer answered, "No, thanks. I buy my oil at Sears. To be honest, they're cheaper."

Then the young gas-station owner got his bright idea: "Cheaper? But do they put it in for you—or do they just sell it to you in a can and you have to go home and put it in yourself? Well, buy your oil at Sears, bring it here, and I'll put it in for you at no charge. It will be my pleasure."

The surprised customer took him up on his generous offer. The word spread. After servicing one customer after another, he slowly began to get gas sales from people who brought their oil and asked him to put it in!

"That built my business! They let me put their car on the rack while I was working; and when I looked up at the bottom of their car as I drained out the old oil, I'd spot other things. I just wanted to be their best friend—and one step ahead of everyone else. I built a great reputation. People knew they could trust me. If I told them they should replace a filter or a belt, they bought it. Offering to put the oil in free opened so many other opportunities.

"I'd never try to sell them anything if they could still get more mileage out of their brake linings or tires. But I'd tell them, 'In another few months you're going to need new tires!' That was honest—and very helpful."

He was on a path to outstanding success and was honored as one of ten extremely successful Americans with his election into the Horatio Alger Association in 1996. He earned that honor.

- He worked harder.
- He worked smarter.
- He worked with a longer look!

As a result, he built a great reputation.

5. **A delay gives many people the opportunity to change for the better.** In other words,

people who are obstructionists today may change their views and become our partners!

If timing is delayed, there's always the possibility of a reconciliation. The end result? A win-win situation. Consider these potential "happy endings":

- Competitors become partners.
- The business is turned around.
- The brokenness is healed.
- The marriage is saved.

"Time wounds all heels and heals all wounds." That old line is still a wise one. Yes, give God time and watch how people change. Consider the following example of nine famous Irishmen.

In the Irish disturbances of 1848, the following nine men were captured, tried, and convicted of treason against Her Majesty the Queen, and were sentenced to death: John Mitchell, Morris Lyene, Patrick Donahue, Thomas McGee, Charles Duffy, Thomas Meagher, Richard O'Gorman, Terrence McManus, and Michael Ireland.

Before passing sentence, the judge asked if there was anything that anyone wished to say. Thomas Meagher, speaking for all, said in effect, "My lord, this is our first offense but not our last. If you'll be easy with us this once, we promise, on our word as gentlemen, to try to do better next time, and next time—sure we won't be fools to get caught."

Thereupon the indignant judge sentenced them all to be hanged by the neck until dead. Passionate protest from all the world forced Queen Victoria to commute the sentence to transportation for life to far-off "wild" Australia.

In 1874, word reached the astounded Queen Victoria that the Sir Charles Duffy who had been elected premier minister of Victoria was the same Charles Duffy who had been transported twenty-five years before. At the queen's demand, the records of the rest of the transported men were revealed. The list that follows shows what had become of the remaining eight men:

Thomas Meagher, governor of Montana

Terrence McManus, brigadier general, United States Army

Patrick Donahue, brigadier general, United States Army

Richard O'Gorman, governor general of Newfoundland

Morris Lyene, attorney general of Australia (in which office Michael Ireland succeeded him)

Thomas McGee, member of parliament, Montreal; minister of agriculture and president of the Council Dominion of Canada

John Mitchell, prominent New York politician (and the father of John Purroy Mitchell, mayor of New York at the outbreak of World War I)

6. **A delay may allow you to get your deal or your act together.** Now you can make trade-offs you weren't prepared to make at the outset; more time makes this possible. Success is often a matter of negotiations, which spell compromise, which is a definition of politics. And good politics is the practice of give-and-take.

As I write these lines, Disneyland in Anaheim, California, has just celebrated its fortieth anniversary. Years ago Disneyland revealed plans for an exciting, major new expansion. Time after time the new project was reported as a go, only to be put on hold—again. The latest news is that it's on again. Disneyland and the city of Anaheim have worked out a successful partnership. Development of the project, which may run into billions of dollars, will be financed with city-sponsored tax-exempt bonds over forty years. Forty years? Now the long time frame for planning makes sense!

7. **A delay may mean that obstructive laws and oppressive regulations can be changed.** Success that comes later—but as a consequence of those changes—may be well worth the wait. Remember the equation we looked at earlier? Passion + Timing = Success.

The July 31, 1996 issue of *USA Today* carried this fantastic story. It took nineteen years for one fifteen-year-old girl to see her dream come true. Dorothy Richardson was a top girl's softball player. When she was only fifteen years old, she was offered a fabulous opportunity to enter the professional softball league. She was put on the protected list for the Connecticut Falcons. But she didn't sign up.

"No," she said. "If I sign on with the Falcons, I'll be a professional, and that would disqualify me from playing in the Olympics."

"But Dot," her close friends reminded her, "softball isn't a part of the Olympics."

"Not yet," she conceded. "But someday it might be. And when that happens, I want to be on the first U.S. team to play softball in the Olympics."

Dorothy pushed herself in high school athletics. She made all-conference in tennis, softball, and track and field at her Orlando, Florida, high school. But her passion was softball. At the age of seventeen she won a gold medal in the Pan American Games (and she went on to win three more in subsequent years). Four times she made all-American, and she was named player of the decade in the eighties. She knew she could make the U.S. Olympic team, if only the International Olympic Committee would accept softball.

Then came 1992. A proposal was presented to the committee to include softball as a demonstration sport for the first time in the Olympics in Barcelona, Spain. No one was more excited than Dorothy. And no one was more crushed than she when the proposal was dropped.

Once more she put the dream aside—but on the back burner, not in the wastebasket. Meanwhile, after her graduation from high school, she pursued another dream: to become a physician.

Thank God for back burners!

"Wait, yes—but don't waste your life while you're waiting," a little voice told her. She enrolled at UCLA to pursue her dream of becoming an orthopedic surgeon. Though scholastics were her focus, her passion for softball had her playing (and winning player-of-the-year awards) all four of her years at UCLA. And upon graduation she won a scholarship to Louisville Medical School, where she earned her medical degree. Now an M.D., the young doctor applied and was accepted for a five-year residency in orthopedics at USC. She was ready to move on from softball to her chosen career.

The year was 1995. Dr. Richardson had finished her first year of her residency when she heard the news: the International Olympic Committee had voted to make softball a full-medal-status event at the 1996 Olympic Games in Atlanta, Georgia.

Too late for her? Not if she played the possibility-thinking game! Could USC possibly be influenced to give her a year's leave of absence from her residency program? Would Ralph Raymond, the U.S. softball coach, work around her schedule? Did she still have what it takes— going on thirty-four years of age—in this young girl's sport? Yes, yes, and yes!

Columbus, Ohio, was the site chosen for Olympic softball training. Abandon medicine for a year? Not quite. Twice while in Olympic training she assisted in surgery at the Hughston Clinic in Columbus. Off went the softball uniform; on went the doctor's mask and green surgical gown. One procedure she helped with was a capsular shift; the second procedure was arthroscopic knee surgery.

Out of the hospital after one of these procedures, she raced to the team's practice. She was late—the team was already in the second inning —but the coach put her straight into the game.

It's now some months later, and she's in Atlanta, Georgia. The U.S. team is playing Australia. The game is tied one to one at the end of the ninth inning. During the tenth inning, Australia hits a home run and wins.

Dr. Richardson checks her scraped arms— par for a shortstop who flies through the air in a dive for second base, catching the Australian runner out. But the loss isn't critical. The U.S. team is still leading in the games five to one.

They've already clinched one of four medal-round shots before this defeat. No tears over this one loss. She's saving her tears for a more important day: the day of the medal ceremonies—when the gold belongs to her team.

In the history of the Olympics, Dorothy Richardson is on record as having played in the first competition to feature softball—and having won the gold medal!

8. **A delay means I'm not finished yet.** You'll never quit as long as you have some time left!

My favorite spectator sport is football. I've never played it, except from the stands. Over the course of my forty years in California, I've seen many a great game. I can think of no game in my lifetime to match the 1982 game between the California Golden Bears and their archrival from Stanford.

It was the last minute of the game. The score? Golden Bears nineteen, Stanford seventeen. The Golden Bears were winning—had almost guaranteed the win—when the awesome Cardinals did the incredible. They made a field goal that put them in the lead (twenty to nineteen) with only seconds left. The Stanford marching band took their places in the end zone, assuming victory. With four seconds left, Stanford kicked. The Bears received, took the ball through Stanford's defense, passed laterally (once, twice, three times, four times, five times), and hurtled into the end zone and the rival team's band. Touchdown! The score: Golden Bears twenty-five, Cardinals twenty. When the California football coach, Joe Kapp, was asked how his team could have imagined going for a win with only four seconds left to score after receiving a kickoff, he said, "The game is sixty minutes, not fifty-nine minutes and fifty-six seconds."

9. A delay recognizes that the future can be your best friend.

From the dying former vice-president of the United States, Hubert H. Humphrey, I heard for the first time a message that would become important to me. His hollow eyes twinkled as he prepared to read to me. "Listen to these words, Bob," he said.

"The future has several names.
For the weak it is 'Impossible'
For the fainthearted it is 'Unknown'
For the thoughtful and valiant it is 'Ideal.'"

"Then for you, Hubert," I said, "the future is ideal. You must go back to Washington for one last hurrah!" And he did!

The future is ideal.

So you lost the game? There's another season next year. So you had a crop failure? But you got your seeds back in the puny pickings at harvest time.

An old Chinese proverb: "In no prairie fires do the seeds perish. Watch the blades shoot forth among the spring breezes."

All the flowers of summer owe everything to the seeds of spring.

Timing—delayed by disaster? But there's always something left. Burned to the ground? Perhaps, but the land was left. The ground never burns.

Richard Neutra designed and built one of the twentieth century's most recognized houses —his own—on what many would call an impossibly tiny lot. The address: 2300 Silver Lake Boulevard, Los Angeles, California. Here the famous architect made history with radiant heating and sliding-glass doors that would earn him the A.I.A. gold medal for innovative, creative design. The house would earn a permanent place in history.

I spent many days and evenings in that house. Then one morning the telephone rang. On the other end was a distraught Richard Neutra. "It's all gone, Bob! My house burned, and I lost everything in it. Pictures. Documents. Unpublished papers. I have nothing left. I'm finished as an architect."

I'd helped him through depression more than once when he'd faced much lesser difficulties. We'd often discussed Freud's insight that in every person there's "the will to live and the will to die." And Neutra had had more than one battle with the will to die. I know: I prayed him through. Now I wasn't concerned about the loss of his home, but I didn't want the world to lose a great architect (or me to lose a good friend).

"But the lot is still there, and that's a lot left," I pointed out. "You can rebuild and include what you've learned since you designed the first house. You can make the new house an even better one," I challenged.

And Neutra did just that. The second house was a perfect reproduction, built on the same foundation on the same lot. But it was better than the first one—not in style but in strength. For example, in the rebuilt home sturdy steel beams replaced the wooden beams that had showed a tendency to warp.

I was invited to the open house. Richard was happier than I'd ever seen him. He was once more filled with enthusiasm and felt a renewed dedication to his chosen career. He didn't quit in the dark time. He didn't abandon his career. Instead, he was so renewed in spirit following the rebuilding that he agreed to design for our church the Tower of Hope.

"I want a lighted cross at the top," I said. "My dream is to have America's first twenty-four-hour crisis-intervention telephone ministry housed in that tower. Here we'll train hundreds of volunteers to answer the telephones and encourage persons who are in crisis—even suicidal."

He sketched what stands today—the Tower of Hope. It's a monument that's an instrument of inspiration. The lights never go out in this structure. For discouraged persons experiencing disappointing delays, we've built a shining, silent beacon that sends a message of hope to a discouraged world. And in that beacon we installed the free crisis-intervention counseling line that had been my dream.

September 16, 1968. The lights went on in the Tower of Hope, and the New Hope telephone started ringing. For over a quarter-century people—numbering in the millions—have dialed this number: area code 714 and the seven saving letters—N-E-W-H-O-P-E. New Hope is alive and alert, handling troubled and troubling calls with compassion. The lights have never gone out in this Tower of Hope.

So the shining, silent sermon sent out from this Tower of Hope is really true:

> There's a light that never goes out . . .
> There's an eye that never closes . . .
> There's an ear that's never shut . . .
> There's a heart that never grows cold.
>
> Wait, I say, on the Lord, and
> He shall strengthen your heart [Psalm 27:14].
>
> Those who wait on the Lord will mount
> up with wings like eagles. They shall
> walk and not faint. They shall run
> and never grow weary [Isaiah 40:31].

10. **A delay means that you have a chance to try again.**

Meet another one of my heroes and dear friends and read his story as he shared it on the *Hour of Power* program.

Norman Vaughan is impeccable in his timing. In the 1920s, when he was a student at Harvard, he read this advertisement in the paper: "Planning a risky trip to the South Pole. If successful, we will be the first persons in history to reach this frozen point of the globe. I need dog-sled drivers." Immediately Norman dropped everything and applied to be a dog-sled driver for Admiral Byrd. He made the draw and joined the expedition. He was such an important part of the history-making exploration that Byrd named a snow-covered mountain in the Antarctic region Mount Vaughan. And this launched a lifetime career for the young man in his early twenties.

During World War II Colonel Vaughan served in a U.S. Army Air Corps Search and Rescue unit, with four hundred and twenty-five dogs under his command. During the Battle of the Bulge, Colonel Vaughan, with his dogs and drivers, controlled the dog-sled ambulances that rescued wounded soldiers. He also single-handedly retrieved a top-secret Norden bombsight before Hitler could grab it.

He would race the Iditarod thirteen times and become the oldest person (at the age of eighty-five) to run this famous twenty-seven-mile race, alone with his dogs and sled on Alaska's winter path.

The year is 1977. Colonel Vaughan is listening to the news in his Anchorage home. Jimmy Carter has just been elected president. A gala presidential parade will lead Carter to the installation ceremony in front of the White House. In that parade—now only eight days away—most of the states will have an entry, but not Alaska.

"Now!" Colonel Vaughan exclaimed. Impulsively, positively, Colonel Vaughan picked up the telephone and called a friend who owned a truck. "I need your help," he urged. "Come over immediately and take me, with my sled and dogs, to Washington, D.C. We're going to represent Alaska in the presidential parade next week!"

Anchorage to Washington by truck. Could they make it in only a few days? Yes!

Colonel Vaughan, no longer a young man, met one of his senators in Washington. "Senator, Alaska must be in that parade," he said persuasively. "I've got my dogs and my sled. Let me represent our great state!"

The senator called in his secretary, explained the situation, and asked her to call the parade headquarters. Minutes later she returned. "Sorry, Senator. The parade entries were all set weeks ago. You can't get in without a number. There are forty-eight numbers, and all numbers are assigned."

Colonel Vaughan raised himself to his full height and said with authority, "Call them back and tell them I've got number forty-eight and a half!"

She turned abruptly and left the room. Moments later she returned with excitement and said proudly, "Senator, Alaska is in! We've been assigned number forty-eight and a half."

Before a worldwide audience, Colonel Vaughan—with dogs and sled—proudly paraded down Pennsylvania Avenue representing Alaska that bright, beautiful morning!

Years later, when Colonel Vaughan was in his late eighties, was he enjoying a sedentary retirement? No more dreams for the sunset years? On the contrary, an impossible expedition was taking shape in this old man's mind: "Mount Vaughan at the South Pole has never been climbed. I'll be the first to do it—just before I turn ninety!"

It took at least a year to get his expedition planned and outfitted. Once the groundwork had been laid, sled and dogs had to be flown from Alaska to a South American airport. Another plane carried his cargo—tent, dog food, and supplies. From South America—once all the preparations were complete and the weather looked favorable—he and his party would continue to the South Pole.

The date was selected—prayerfully—and the expedition double-checked its preparations while waiting. On the precise date he'd planned, Colonel Vaughan reached the Antarctic. A smaller plane waited to take him and his live cargo of dogs to the foot of the mountain. He would make it! He would stand at the top of Mount Vaughan on his eighty-ninth birthday!

Finally they felt ready for the ten-thousand-foot climb, to the top of Mount Vaughan. But timing was critical. They had to wait for the narrow window when the chances of blinding blizzards would be minimized.

They were airborne! Then suddenly—the accident happened. Everyone survived—both he and his dogs lived through the plane crash—but the window of time disappeared. There would be no way now to reach the mountain in time. "Next year," Colonel Vaughan said. "Yes, we'll get everything together and we'll go back and climb that mountain!"

One year later he packed again. He got as far as the foot of his mountain. The dogs were well and anxious. So was he. Huddled in his heavy winter garb, his head lost deep in the furry helmet, snowshoes buckled, he flashed his famous smile and barked a command to his best friends: his dogs. "Let's climb the mountain!" he shouted. "I want to stand up there tomorrow to celebrate my ninetieth birthday!"

And he did it! All the world watched the climb to the top of Mount Vaughan at the South Pole by ninety-year-old Colonel Vaughan, filmed by National Geographic Television. "Happy birthday, to my dear friend, Colonel Vaughan!"

11. **A delay gives God a chance to take over.**

So important is timing in the architecture of successful living that one of the Ten Commandments deals with time management: "Remember the Sabbath to keep it holy" (Exodus 20:8). Tradition carries on this truth learned from experience by preceding generations. One day in seven, you should plan to retreat, relax, and regroup as a family. Review, reload, and prepare for reentry on Monday morning. Reconnect with God and faith.

Take time to fill your spiritual fuel tank with gas. Tomorrow is Monday. You don't want to take off on an empty tank. Remember?

I'm convinced that people who discipline themselves to take one day a week to refuel their emotional gas tank will keep their energy up. Stop on Sunday to recharge your positive mental attitude in your place of positive meditation. God sends creative ideas into minds that open up in quiet prayer and meditation, letting the subconscious know it's protected from uninvited, pressure-producing interruptions.

The timing may be delayed. And we must be emotionally prepared to put a positive spin on that!

So stop and pray. Time out! Check your connections with God. Is this new venture why you were born? Is this daring dream God's purpose for your life? Yes, the price in success will include expenditures of time and effort as well as money. But don't be surprised to look back and see that the toughest problem was "waiting for the moment."

Dealing with delays? You did it! You didn't quit, walk away, throw in the towel. Timing— it's everything!

So plan to stay. Hang in there!

Just never, never, never quit! If you quit, you'll be abandoning the base you've built, and then what? You'll never be satisfied, pleased, or content if you quit doing and being what started out as real pleasure. Welcome delays.

They may be God's gifts of grace, increasing your chances of eventual success with a smile.

Look back! See how many good things have happened to you since you were born. Add up all your accomplishments from all your yesterdays, and you'll be surprised to see you've come from nowhere to somewhere.

Look around! See how many good things are happening to you today.

Look ahead! Imagine how many good things can happen in all of your tomorrows—if you'll only keep the faith!

I believe that our greatest temptation is a failure to learn the wisdom of taking "the longer look."

Timing. Is it stressful without faith? You bet it is! But real faith is a force far more powerful than stress.

Do you feel the weight of timing? Let me help you with those pressures.

Don't ever drop the curtain on tomorrow! God's delays aren't God's denials. No, God answers every prayer. I've often said . . .

If the request isn't right,
  His answer is no.
If the timing isn't right,
  His answer is slow.

Winners

never

turn

delays

into

denials.

If you aren't ready—yet—
  His answer is grow.
When everything's right and ready,
  His answer is go!

I was facing a real challenge in my ministry. I had invested more time and more money into a project that wasn't working out as I planned and hoped. I prayed and then heard one sentence clearly in my mind: "Leave it to Me." It was one of the greatest gifts God had ever given me. I was able to turn it over to God and experience total, complete, beautiful peace of mind.

Just last week I was waiting at an airline counter in Chicago. Out of the corner of my eye I noticed a man staring at me. He almost seemed to be waiting to talk to me, although I didn't know him. As I turned to leave, hurrying to catch my plane, he put a friendly hand on my arm. "Dr. Schuller," he said, "I won't take much of your time. But you saved my career eighteen years ago with one sentence. I was going to quit my job. My career was failing. But then I heard you say, 'Inch by inch, anything's a cinch.' That was all I needed. I came up with a new ten-year goal, and I now make over two hundred thousand dollars a year. That's all I wanted to say. That and thank you. Go catch your plane."

God promises to bless us, but He never promises when. Two questions God never answers are "Why?" and "When?" For these questions provoke argument, not acceptance. "Wait on the Lord and He shall strengthen your heart." Yes, power comes to the persons who prevail in patience. Such a person is Tom Harken, my friend. Tom Harken, from Beaumont, Texas, shared with me his frightening delay because of his struggle with adult illiteracy. It would take him years and years before he would learn to read and write . . .

There were days when my illiteracy would really shake me up. One of the most graphic examples came shortly after we'd moved to Beaumont. The parents of my wife, Melba, had become ill, and we needed to travel to their home in Hobart, Oklahoma, to care for them.

It was a long journey, nearly six hundred miles north of Beaumont.

At some point along the way, I said,

"You know, as soon as we're positive your parents are okay, I've got to go back and earn some money to pay the bills. I can't stay unless it's absolutely necessary."

"I understand that," Melba said.

"If I do go back, I'm a little worried about being able to find my way through Dallas," I told her haltingly. "Will you draw me a map or something?"

"Sure, honey, don't worry about it," she said. "You'll be all right."

Back in those days, there were no by-passes, or loops, around cities. You had to drive right through the heart of town, no matter how big it was.

My concern was well-founded. I couldn't read, remember? Street and highway signs really gave me a problem, and Miss Melba was always such a help. After we arrived and found her parents were not too bad, Melba decided to remain there for a few days. I kissed them goodbye and headed back late that evening in order to be back in Beaumont by morning to go to work.

When I reached the big interstate on the return trip, I stopped for gas and coffee, then got confused and couldn't find where I was on the map Melba had drawn for me.

And I certainly wasn't going to ask anyone.

I got into the car and drove, hoping something would start to look familiar or match up with my homemade map.

After three or four hours of going around and around, I was frustrated and totally lost. For all I knew I was headed back toward Oklahoma, and the feeling was nothing short of panic. Only those who have experienced it can know how I felt.

This experience really shook me.

At some point, I turned into an all-night diner just as a Highway Patrol car was pulling in. In Texas today, it's called the Department of Public Safety, but back then it was still the Highway Patrol. I approached the officer and hesitantly told him I was lost and trying to find my way out of Dallas on my way to Beaumont.

An affable guy, he tried to be helpful and began naming off streets I should take to get to the main highway heading south.

"Excuse me," I interrupted as politely as I knew how. "I'm going to tell you something I've never told anyone."

"What's that, sir?" he asked. "What's the problem?"

"I can't read," I said, peering down at the parking lot gravel, as embarrassed as I'd ever been. "You're telling me the names of streets to take, and I don't know anything but numbers."

"How in the world did you get here?" he asked incredulously, and I told him about taking the wife and kids to Oklahoma because her mother and father were ill. The way I was cringing, I must have looked guilty or something.

"Let's see your driver's license," he said, not unkindly.

"Driver's license?" I mumbled. "Well, to tell the truth I don't have one."

"You mean you're driving without a license?"

"Yes, sir. I could never pass the test because I can't read!"

"Follow me," he said.

I just knew I was headed for a night in jail and an appearance before some judge the next morning. There goes another day's work, I decided, momentarily entertaining some wild thought of escaping. Even under the circumstances,

I had to laugh at that. I'd probably turn into a dead end, get pulled over, and be in even more trouble. Flashing red lights were already going off in my brain. Obediently, I followed along behind the patrol car.

To my surprise, the officer led me to a truck-stop coffee shop located on a main highway that didn't look at all familiar. We parked, and he motioned for me to join him inside.

I was really shook up, but he ordered coffee and calmly said he had taken care of my problem.

"What do you mean?" I asked.

"I'm going to lead you out to the city limits, and you're about to be on your way to Beaumont," he said. "I've radioed ahead, and a friend of mine on duty in the next county will meet us.

"He'll take you further south, and in the meantime he'll be making radio contact with one of his neighboring officers, who in turn will do the same, and you'll be back in Beaumont before you know it."

I almost fell at this guy's feet, thanking him profusely and saying that because of him I would always love Dallas, Texas.

"I don't know how to tell you this, Mr. Harken," he said. "But you're not in Dallas; you're in Fort Worth."

That was over thirty years ago, and now I can laugh about it, most of the time. Those were difficult years for me. I knew then and there I had to learn to read. It would take a long time, but I finally succeeded.

Faith is a force, not a farce.

Edgar A. Guest said it this way:

Success is failure turned inside out.
The silver tint of the clouds of doubt.
You never can tell how close you are,
It may be near when it seems afar;
So stick to the fight when you're hardest hit.
It's when things seem worst that you
    mustn't quit.

Yes—build and bolster your faith.
Give God time to work it all out.
To trust the Lord means to "wait on God" while you keep your eyes on your goals. Yes, the timing may be delayed, but the course must be stayed!

VII

THE COURSE
MUST BE STAYED

—⚍—

Wow! What a trip you're on. Look what ports of call you've come from already.

Possibilities have been weighed. This was the home port, where this whole trip started. You had a dream. If you could pull it off, it would be . . . okay? Great? Terrific? Fantastic?

You stepped aboard!

Priorities have been swayed. Your second port of call! Something happened here deep inside of you. Your new possibility became a super positive temptation. What happened to you? Your values changed. Suddenly a new, exciting, impossible dream captured your imagination. You embraced a new vision with real value.

"It would be so much fun, if I could do it!" you fantasized. And achievement should be fun. It's no accident that the vast majority of achiev-

Look for something you enjoy and are pretty good at, and go for it.

ers pick a profession that gives them pleasure.

So you did it: you switched your career plans away from a dull, unsatisfying job—a job that wasn't really for you, that you felt driven into by an empty purse or a desire to please your spouse, peers, or parents.

You suddenly came to conceive and believe that what the real you loves to do could be a valid career choice. People would pay you for doing what you'd gladly do for sport!

Your priorities were swayed. Your trip then reached the next port of call, where . . .

Plans have been laid. You challenged the voices that told you your dream was impossible. Confronting the obstacles that negative-thinking experts threw at you, you argued with passion:

But it might be possible if I . . .
But it could be possible after I . . .
But I could make it happen with . . .
But I could pull it off when . . .
It's not possible here—but . . .
It's not possible yet, not now—but . . .

You decided to stay on the ship and navigate the planned course at least as far as the next port of call. Here . . .

Commitments have been made. What happened to you in this port? You decided to try. You set a goal. You shared your impossible decision with someone you admire, respect, and trust. That person encouraged you to move forward.

You felt a surge of energy! Your new life took decisive direction. The passion burned inside of you as you made the decision to go for it.

That decision led you to the next port of call, where . . .

The price had to be paid. Now you suddenly realized that great achievers are simply ordinary persons who are determined to succeed. You saw that extraordinarily successful people are simple souls who resolved to pay the price to get where they want to go. You became convinced that there are no great people; we're all the same. Great people simply aim higher, make decisions that are more daring, and give more willingly of heart, time, and money to reach their goals.

Time out. At the next port of call the timing was delayed. You were told that your endeavor would take longer than scheduled. You ran into frustrations that you didn't expect, plan for, or include in your budget.

You needed—what? More permits? An advanced degree? More money?

You faced a myriad of questions such as

these: How much more would it cost? How long would it take to get your act together? Would you have to relocate? Reorganize? Rehire specialists? Go back to school? Refinance? You told yourself, "I've got to think bigger, think smarter, think longer. I'm heading into the next-to-the-last port. I can't jump ship here or now. I can't walk away, just before the next port!"

I can't think of an achiever who didn't have to go through this port. Every dreamer experiences a time when things aren't moving, when progress is bogged down. I believe that God allows this to happen to prepare us to receive success with profound gratitude and true humility!

The course must be stayed. This is your present port of call. Here you're at a real testing time. Here you confront a loss of enthusiasm. Your energy level is at a dangerous low. The strong winds of passion that have been driving you are no longer filling your sails. You aren't moving ahead anymore. "What should I do?" you ask.

—⚏—

Look up and check the sky sails.

—⚏—

"All sails are set, sir." Many a captain heard that glad sound in the glorious heyday of ocean-going clippers. And wise was the captain who, when he set his schedule, prepared not only for good winds but also for dead seas and storms. During the storms—the trying times we all face—a wise old captain would know that it's not how hard the wind blows that matters, but how strong the mast is and how firmly the sails are tied down.

Then there are the dead seas, with nary a breath of wind. The sails hang limp. The vigorous surge of a fully wind-blown ship is dead. The calm is deadening. Progress is delayed.

Wise captains plan for delays that are out of their control. Look how the old China clippers were designed. First there were the gallant sails, large and strong, to catch the full power of a strong wind. Above them were set smaller sails to catch higher breezes; these were called the royal sails. But above the gallant sails and the royal sails were the sky sails—small and light. Tied to the very top of the tall masts, they were designed to catch the smallest wisp of wind, the slightest, lightest, highest breeze. Although they'd never deliver enough thrust to take the great China clipper across the ocean, they too served a lifesaving purpose: they were enough to keep a becalmed vessel from drifting off course.

Again and again it was the sky sails that saved the day in deadening delays. They didn't move the ship to its port, but they kept the vessel on its course.

CONNECTING WITH THE STAYING-POWER OF POSSIBILITY THINKING

Yes, the course must be stayed, but first I have to figure out where I am. How did I get into this? What have I invested in time, money, energy? What do I do now? What's this pathway to prosperity all about anyway?

I started to play. I got into it because I thought it would be fun. It was fun, and it still could be.

I stopped to pray. I honestly, openly, sincerely connected with the Highest Wisdom before I set my goals and made my decisions.

I prepared to pay. Yes, I worked hard! I sacrificed—blood, sweat, and tears. I didn't look for shortcuts; I paid the price.

Now I've decided to stay and hold fast

through the dead calm or the scary storm. I won't turn back. If I fail, I can be proud and not ashamed. I'll practice what I've always believed: I'd rather attempt to do something great and fail than attempt to do nothing and succeed.

Now that I've decided to stay, to hold fast, I absolutely must check the sky sails. And what does that entail? I must review, reread, and re-dedicate myself to the God-power of possibility thinking. The principles of possibility thinking that follow will help me put a fresh breeze in the sky sails of my soul and keep me on course; they'll catch the feeble breezes and help me keep my eyes on my goal.

1. **Possibility thinkers are WOW thinkers.**
That's what got me where I am today.

I had a dream. Yes, it was impossible. But WOW—what an idea! Even now, as I recall the wallop I felt when the dream hit me, I still say, "WOW—what a great idea that was and still is!"

I mustn't forget the WOW.

2. **Possibility thinkers are HOW thinkers.**
Possibility thinkers follow the WOW with a HOW. If it's a WOW idea, the odds are it'll be

fantastic—but impossible—when it first strikes your mind. Positive assumptions mysteriously begin their march. Possibility thinkers assume that somehow this dream just might be pulled off. They ask HOW it could be made possible. Amazing signals are picked up! The creativity that's unleashed in a WOW idea is enough to inspire the possibility thinker to take an option out on his or her ideas and begin to research HOW it can happen seriously! I've got to get back to "HOW" thinking.

3. **Possibility thinkers are NOW thinkers.**

Possibility thinkers don't procrastinate; they dedicate. They never allow great ideas to fall into black holes. They write every great thought down rather than trusting their memory. They write their WOW ideas in big letters at the top of their to-do list or in their diary, notebook, or journal. Or they pick up the telephone and delegate a particular idea to a look-into-it-and-report-back-to-me person. They try to find out whether they can secure the possibility with an option to buy. Can they assign the possibility to an associate who's gifted in research? Can they delegate the opportunity to a make-it-happen person?

"I'm a NOW thinker," you affirm. "I make risky—even scary—decisions! I won't let a good opportunity pass me by. I'll grab hold of it! I'm alive, alert! NOW! There's someone I can talk to. There's a new idea waiting to come into my thinking that could make a difference! I'm open to God for a breakthrough insight.

4. **Possibility thinkers are VOW thinkers.**

Possibility thinkers make decisions. They make determined commitments. I did. I made promises to myself, my family, my friends, and my God; and I can't break those promises. I can live with honest failures, but I can't live with shameful broken promises. "Leave it to me," God whispers in my ear. If God wants to let a dream die, then He'll have to make the failure happen. I can live with that.

So I've practiced all of this. WOW thinking. HOW thinking. NOW thinking. VOW thinking. What more can I do? What? Yes! I never thought of this before!

5. **Possibility thinkers are PLOW thinkers.**

Possibility thinkers are prepared to dig deep, break ground, and work—longer, harder, smarter! Yes, work.

Of course! Jesus said it: "No man having put his hand to the plow and looking back, is fit for the kingdom of God" (Luke 9:62).

Here's how possibility thinkers make it happen. They break new ground and begin with a revived vision. They don't look back; they know there's nothing for them anymore in yesterday. They look ahead. There's something there, waiting for them in the tomorrows.

And that refreshed vision gives them bright new light and life. "Where there is no vision the people perish" (Proverbs 29:18, KJV). They may see tough problems coming out of the shadows, but quitting isn't a part of their plan at this stage.

—∞—

If it's going to be, it's up to me!

—∞—

Let me share a true story. It's the inspiring story of my friend Chuck Wall. He's been a listener to my television talks for many, many years. He understands possibility thinking, and he lives it!

Dr. Chuck Wall, a full-time professor at Bakersfield College, is a WOW thinker, a HOW thinker, a NOW thinker, a VOW thinker, and a PLOW thinker. He has retinitis pigmentosa and is legally blind. Chuck teaches management courses, including "Human Relations and Motivation." Chuck holds to the theory that while many people become technically knowledgeable in a given field, unless and until they can get along with others, they're not going to be as successful as they would like. So he spends much of his time preparing business students for the multicultural society in business today.

About two years ago Chuck, like millions of other people around the world, became (he told me) "completely fed up with the incredible amount of violence in the newspaper. Listening to the radio or watching television has become nothing more than a tour through murder, rape, massacre, and assorted mayhem that tends to depress and demoralize us."

One morning as Chuck was preparing for his classes at Bakersfield College, he overheard a radio announcer say, "Today we have another random act of senseless violence to report." And Chuck thought, "Violence—is that all this world can talk about? Isn't there anything else that can encourage us? Is there no good news?" But then he started thinking about the phrase he'd just heard, and he had a WOW thought: "What if I took out the word violence and put in the word kindness? I would take a very well known negative phrase and turn it into a positive one, and out of that could come a great assignment for my students."

So that morning, Dr. Wall walked into his classroom to share his new assignment with his students. He asked them to write down their task: "Today I'll go out into my community and commit at least one random act of senseless . . . "—he waited for them to catch up with him—"kindness!" And they all exclaimed as one voice, "What?" One student asked, "Is this going to count toward our grade? How much is it worth?" Another asked, "Does it have to be typed?" Still another said, "And by the way, please define kindness for us." Chuck refused to do that, because he wanted to see in this assignment what his students believed kindness to be. His only further instruction was that the assignment was due in two weeks.

Chuck was inspired by his students. One, a woman named Sharon (name changed) who'd been out of school for some years, took her eight-year-old daughter to visit patients at a convalescent hospital. They walked up and down the corridors offering encouragement to patients. She wrote, "I don't know who benefited most from this experience—my daughter and I or the patients—but it's immaterial now.

This is part of our quality time together. We plan to visit hospitals every week."

Another student, a young man of nineteen named Carlos (name changed), overheard his mother say to a friend on the telephone, "I've just received my utility bill, and I don't know where the money is going to come from to pay it. I'm really afraid they're going to turn off the electricity." Carlos went to the bank, withdrew money from his own personal account—savings from his summer job—went to the utility office, and paid the bill. He took a stamped receipt home to a very grateful and proud mom.

Another student, Sara (name changed), found a very disheveled collie wandering around her neighborhood. She took the dog home and gave it a bath. Then she put some posters around the neighborhood showing the dog's picture. She soon found the owner, who was very, very pleased to get his dog back.

And how about Ashley (name changed), who found the last parking spot in a huge, crowded parking lot? Gratefully she started to pull in, only to look in her rear view mirror and see the woman in the car behind her throwing up her hands in sheer frustration, as if to say, "Where am I going to park?" Ashley backed out of the parking spot and waved the woman in. The recipient of the spot looked amazed; she couldn't believe this was actually happening. Ashley had to park about a quarter-mile away, but she reported, "You know, I smiled for three days."

Chuck has received over fifteen thousand letters and phone calls at his Bakersfield College office and has completed about two hundred media interviews. At first he thought the acts-of-kindness crusade was a fad, but people still call and write letters describing their own acts of kindness and talking about how there's renewed hope in this world. As Chuck says, "Maybe kindness isn't the answer to all of our world's problems, but it's where we have to start. There's nothing new about this concept. We've just forgotten it, and now it's time to remember.

"Challenge all of your readers to participate in this acts-of-kindness crusade. Nothing gets done of a positive nature until each one of us personally gets involved. We don't have to wait for a governmental decree to be made to realize that what you and I want in our lives is the same thing that everyone else wants, and that's respect and dignity. I want it. You want it. So I challenge you to participate and become active. Today I'll commit one random act of senseless kindness. Will you?"

Chuck Wall, with his blindness, could be bitter and filled with self-pity; instead, he bubbles with enthusiasm about life, his marriage, and his career. Because Chuck is a possibility-thinking Christian—someone who's been introduced to that wonderful person, Jesus Christ—goodness emanates from Christ into his mind and heart.

Yes, that's how possibility thinking works to keep the ship on course. Possibility thinkers are WOW, HOW, NOW, VOW, and PLOW thinkers! The course will be stayed.

TURNING A DREAMER INTO A SELF-MOTIVATOR

Failure doesn't happen until you make the decision to quit.

People can block you. Friends can overprotect you. Forces may frustrate you. Enemies may obstruct you. Families may discourage you. But only you and you alone can defeat yourself.

No other person—no one but you—has the power to destroy your dream. You're responsible if it's dead, buried, finished, over. Your signature alone can sign the death certificate of your dream.

Turn yourself into your best friend and biggest booster! How?

Be a super self-motivator!

"Fine," you say, "but how do I do that?" Listed below are the eight most powerful words I can share with you. They're self-motivating words. Read them. Memorize them. Soak your soul in them. If you affirm these eight words, the course will be stayed! Do so now, and remember: "If it's going to be, it's up to me!"

- I am
- I can
- I will
- I believe

These four powerful self-affirmations turn the dreamer into a self-motivator.

To stay on your course, you need to focus on self-affirmation! Keep affirming your worth and value to yourself, to your team, and to your clients and customers. This is the time to toot your own horn. Wise business owners know that they must sing their own praises! Their competitors surely won't! And people forget too quickly how great you really are.

"If it's going to be, it's up to me!"

Read—aloud—these sentences:

I am an asset—for someone, somewhere.

I am going to be noticed. Some good job will find me, if I don't give up looking and working for it.

I am going to stand out—in some way! As a performer, or as a producer, or as a person.

I am changing. Growing. Improving! I know that when I'm no longer changing, I'm through.

I am now a decision-making, goal-setting, God-connected person.

I am succeeding already, for I'm into new insights and new motivation. I'm on a good track.

I am turning my back on mediocrity and my face toward excellence.

I am free—free to shape my future. I have the God-given liberty to choose my destiny. I won't be diverted.

I am walking away from depressing memories. I am planning to create delightful and inspiring new memories! I'll make the most of what's coming and the least of what's gone.

I am setting great and good goals and will pay the price.

I am encountering challenges. WOW! I am going to creatively confront frustrations—and yes, disappointments and adversities—but I shall never abandon my ultimate God-inspired goals!

I am taking control of my life. I shall no longer be intimidated and manipulated by cynical, negative, unbelieving, jealous faces or factors.

I am building a winning team. I am in the most important game of my life. I'm going to check my position. Check the challengers and the challenge. Check the clock and the scoreboard. Do I call for a time-out, a huddle, or a special play?

I am becoming a beautiful human being. I'll stop making waves and start making ways.

I am! I can!

Congratulations! You're a different and a better you than you were when you first opened this book! You have a new picture of yourself. You now see yourself not as a nobody or a has-been but as a somebody in the process of becoming. That's great! Take comfort in these words: "The me I see is the me I'll be!"

"You are the light of the world."

"You are the salt of the earth."

These affirmations are from Jesus Christ. If He believes that strongly in you, then you can believe in yourself too.

Jesus Christ knows you even if you don't know Him. You may not yet have found the faith, but I have fantastic news:

A faith has found you!

You're a spiritual being on a human journey.

The late René Dubos, famed sociobiologist, said that the greatest problem facing our world today isn't found in the popular academic lists. It's not thermonuclear war, overpopulation, or negative environmental developments, to name a few. None of these is the greatest problem, he said, explaining his deeper insight: "The greatest problem is that the human being will lose the faith that he can manage to overcome those problems."

The solution to the biggest problem? "I am" and "I can!" Powerful, positive self-esteem is what we all need. So to make yourself part of the solution, reinvigorate your self-confidence. Give your self-esteem a boost.

Dr. David Burns is recognized as one of the most esteemed psychiatrists of the late twentieth century. He and I have done work together on this subject of self-esteem. He agrees with me that one of the deepest needs in a human being is the spiritual hunger for the divine dignity that's our birthright as creatures designed in the image of God.

Thirty years ago I published my flagship book, *Move Ahead with Possibility Thinking*. It's worked wonders for many persons and been a failure with others. "Why doesn't everyone find it helpful?" I asked myself. And eventually I found the answer. In talking with people after that book's publication, I learned that those who suffered from low self-esteem couldn't believe in possibility thinking. My answer to them? A follow-up book entitled *Self-Love: The Dynamic Force of Success.* It too worked beautifully for those who had a positive spiritual attitude. For those without a vital faith, I wrote the next book, *Self-Esteem: The New Reformation* (subtitled *A Theology of Self-Esteem*).

Before I published that theology of self-esteem, I retained the esteemed researcher George Gallup to assist me; I used his sources and resources to study the subject of self-esteem sociologically in the United States of America. His report was phenomenal. Let me share some of what I learned from that Gallup research.

1. **People with high self-esteem don't tend to get angry.** Self-control is a very important virtue. To be an achiever, you'll need to build a team, and teamwork requires control. Frustration-inducing events will always be there. Those who have poor self-esteem will act on their frustration, while those with high self-esteem will keep cool even in a panic. So self-

esteem is all-important! Take strength from this affirmation: "I can—if I can keep calm and creative."

2. **People with high self-esteem are resilient.** They tend to have incredible power to come back repeatedly from the most unimaginable negative experiences. "I can—if I have bouncebackability."

3. **People with high self-esteem are more highly productive in work-per-hour output.** They put a lot more effort out in less time than others, and they tend to commit themselves to doing a really great job in whatever they're doing. They take pride in their work. Fantastic! Their "I can" spirit is proven in their productivity.

4. **People with high self-esteem are less likely than others to abuse alcohol, chemicals, and drugs.** Even legal drugs, prescribed by doctors, Dr. Gallup reported, are less addictive to people who have healthy self-esteem. Young people who fail to develop strong self-esteem in school, in their community, in their family, and in their church believe that they're no good; they feel that they "can't do it," and to escape their insecurity they turn to chemicals.

5. **Finally, persons with a strong, healthy spiritual self-esteem always seem to find "a**

way out of no way," to use the title of my friend Andrew Young's new book. He's battled racism all of his life. No one was closer to Martin Luther King, Jr., than he. "I can"—these two words drive him.

No matter who you are: keep your life's purpose on course. Fulfill your mission. You're a child of God, and you can be an achiever!

You shrug and say, "Oh, I'm just a brick-layer. I never went to school, never went to college. I . . . I'm nothing."

I was inspired years ago when someone sent me a copy of a German laborer's will. He was a poor mason, but he felt pride in his workmanship as he mixed cement and cut the stones. When he died, in his will were these words: "I leave to my eldest son my most prized possession: a tool I used to cut the stones in the Cologne Cathedral."

Mother Teresa personally gave me her familiar blessing: "Be someone . . . for somebody!" And now I pass it on to you. You're alive; you're a human being. You're not just a biological accident, unwanted, unvalued. Somebody needs you!

When my daughter Carol had her leg amputated and had to be in the hospital for seven painful months, she used to say that she made it through the lonely and painful days because of the cleaning girl. The cleaning girl? Yes, a little Vietnamese girl whose family had escaped Vietnam and come to America. She could speak little English. No one had wanted to hire her because she was unqualified—except to do a job nobody wanted: emptying the wastebaskets in a hospital. You never know what's in a hospital wastebasket. You might pick up a germ that could kill you. Yes, she wore the plastic gloves, but every time she entered Carol's room she stopped just a minute and smiled. Then she went to the wastebasket, picked it up, and smiled again at the thirteen-year-old amputee before walking out. Day after day that loving smile gave Carol the strength to stay alive and not give up. And we don't even know the girl's name.

Perhaps she thought, "I can smile, even if I can't speak a foreign language, for I'm somebody!"

Corrie ten Boom was a Dutch woman who was sent by Hitler to a death camp to live and die with the Jews. How she escaped was a miracle of God. I knew her well. She attended my church the last years of her life; and when she became too ill to attend church, I visited her at her bedside to serve her Communion, giving her the blessing in her own Dutch language.

Corrie often came to visit Carol in the hospital after the accident—sometimes daily, before she herself became ill. "You must fight on!" she would say in her thick Dutch accent. "You can! Yes, you can!" She became Carol's warrior. She was as essential to Carol's recovery as were all the medical experts and the little Vietnamese cleaning girl. Each time Corrie came, she gave Carol her blessing: "Remember, no person is too small for God's love, and no problem is too big for God's power."

Mother Teresa, Corrie ten Boom, George Gallup, David Burns—I could go on and on and on, but let me quote another writer. His name is Robert Schuller. He wrote one of his best lines when he was going from Gorba–chev's to Yeltsin's office in the Kremlin. Riding through Moscow, he thought, "Communism is dead. They think they're free." Then suddenly he was hit with this line: "I'm not free till I believe in me!"

Self-esteem is now recognized as a very dynamic human quality. That's the result of quite a revolution over the past twenty years. Yet many secularists who are on the self-esteem bandwagon reject the spiritual reality of the human being.

Let it be said, it's not a mark of intelligence or well-rounded education to totally ignore the Bible. No self-esteem can match the "I am" and the "I can" power that's revealed in these holy words from Psalm 139:

Oh, Lord, You have searched me and known me. You know my sitting down and my rising up. You understand my thoughts afar off.

If I stand in heaven, You are there. If I make my bed in hell, behold, You are there. If I take the wings of the morning and dwell in the uttermost parts of the sea, even there shall Your hand lead me and hold me. You formed my inward parts. You have covered me in my mother's womb. I will praise You for I am brilliantly and wonderfully made. Marvelous are your works.

Read all the self-esteem literature you can, but until you connect with your Creator—God—you're missing the natural, normal connection humans were designed to experience. You need a solid, unshakable foundation for your "I am" and your "I can" spirit.

I am! I can! I will!

I will do what only I can and must do.

I will take charge. I will take control. I will assume leadership.

And what is leadership? It's the force that selects my dreams, sets my goals, and keeps my mission on course. I will be that force.

With the help of these affirmations, and others listed below, get ready to equip yourself with the dynamic qualities of leadership. The instructions are clear. Read and reread these affirmations again and again. The pilot reads his checklist every time before he takes off. Tomorrow, the next day, and the next. You should too.

1. **I will challenge my "disadvantage complex,"** which I have pathetically and pitifully (and sometimes wrongly) believed. "I'm too old." "I'm too poor." "My skin isn't the right color." "I don't belong to the right political party." "I don't know anybody who's important."

2. **I will rearrange, realign, or restructure my relationships.** I will have the courage to

316

leave the intimacy of those people who are destructive to my self-respect. I will be attracted and get attached to positive people who encourage and motivate me.

3. **I will adopt a positive fitness program for my mind.** If I don't exercise, the muscles atrophy. Likewise, I must feed my mind positive nutrition instead of negative junk food.

4. **I will connect with my Creator, God!** "God loves me! God loves you, and so do I." That's the creed that all members of the Crystal Cathedral congregation learn. Let me suggest that you may need a revision. First affirm, "God loves me, and so will I." Now try the original line: "God loves you, and so do I!"

5. **I will not allow a lack of resources to dissuade me** from the course I've set for my goal.

6. **I will not be intimidated** into silence and retreat.

7. **I will not be manipulated** by prejudices, cultural or racial.

8. **I will challenge the boundaries that would limit my goals and dreams.** I will not allow ceilings to lower my thinking. I will fence out rather than being fenced in.

9. **I will not allow frustrations to make me cash in, give up, throw in the towel, and quit.**

317

I'm living under new orders from my Higher Power. Those orders tell me, "If it's going to come true, it's up to you." To which I respond, "I am; I can; I will."

10. **I will not indulge in negative fantasies** that distract, depress, defuse, or defocus my attention, thereby taking me off course.

11. **I will face my fear of failure** and accomplish something wonderful anyway.

12. **I will manage my energy flow so that fatigue won't overtake me.** I will retreat as needed, taking time out to think and rest so that I don't make bad decisions out of exhaustion.

13. **I will not allow problems, pressures, or pain to become an excuse for quitting.** I will honestly face and accept my faults and shortcomings and rise above them.

14. **I will not allow negative forecasts, facts, and statistics to get the best of me.** I will not let them depress or discourage me or distract me from my dream.

15. **I will maintain control,** and with God's help I will stay cool, calm, collected, and convicted when I get into a frenzied, frantic situation.

16. **I will reject all fatalism, regardless of its source.** God has put me in charge of my destiny.

17. **I will listen with caution to my opponents and foes** if they can come up with better ideas, especially if they're as interested in seeing me succeed as I am.

18. **I will listen respectfully to the counsel of my most trusted friends,** but the final decision must, and will, be my responsibility.

19. **I will let my hopes lead me.** I will not surrender leadership to my hurts.

20. **I will let my faith be in control of every decision I make and every action I take.** God is in control of my future. I don't know what the future holds, but I know who holds my future.

—∞—

I am! I can!
I will! I believe!

—∞—

These eight words are absolutely life-changing. Say them aloud again: I am! I can! I will! . . . I believe!

The chairman of my board of trustees is a man named Beurt SerVaas. A resident of the Midwest, he was elected president of the Indianapolis city council every year for over thirty-one years in a row! During those thirty-one years, Beurt SerVaas helped transform that town into a world-class city. And he's one of the greatest friends I have. Not only is he successful in business, but he earned his doctorate in medical physiology. At a recent board meeting, he said, "In my medical studies, I've seen many human brains. But I've never seen a human mind."

And he never will. You can't see your mind. It's invisible. You can cut through the brain and examine its various sections, but you can't find and see the mind. It's invisible. But it's real! It's a spiritual scientific reality. Here in the mind resides "soul power." It's yours to claim! Yes, you can be a believer. And just think what "soul power" will be released!

Become a believer and focus on the future. Your course will be stayed as you affirm your personal beliefs in your dream and, more important, in your own self. The following affirmations should help you strengthen your trust in your own ambitions:

1. **I believe that my ambition is the Divine Drive within me.** "It is God at work in me giving me the will and the power to achieve His purpose" (Philippians 2:13). I will honor and welcome the divine desires that impassion me!

2. **I believe in my ambition.** What I feel isn't a vain ambition; therefore, I have no guilt about it. The laborer is worthy of his hire. When I faithfully employ my talent and my time, I can expect a just return for my endeavors. This need won't lead me to selfishness but to stewardship, for I believe that "the earth is the Lord's, the world, and they that dwell therein."

3. **I believe that I must accomplish something worthwhile with the one life I have.** I owe this to parents, family, friends, and teachers. I've received so much. I must give something back before I die.

We are not here to dream, to drift,
we have hard work to do and loads to lift,
shun not the struggle, 'tis God's gift.

                                                    Anonymous

The Old Testament writer of Ecclesiastes wrote, "It is God's gift to everyone that they should eat and drink and take pleasure in all work" (Ecclesiastes 3:13).

4. **I believe that I was born to greatness with a mind capable of thinking and a soul capable of believing in God.**

In a recent radio interview I was asked, "Dr. Schuller, you have a successful and large ministry, but you came from just a little Iowa farm. Doesn't your success surprise you?"

"Not at all," I answered. "I was born to greatness."

The interviewer looked surprised. "What do you mean? Your father wasn't rich."

"No."

"Your parents weren't in the social upper class."

"No."

"What do you mean, then, by saying you were born to greatness?"

I replied, "To begin with, I was born on a farm. There I learned responsibility. I had chores to do, and I had to do them. Whatever the weather! Whatever the problems! Whatever the pain! Whatever the risk! The cows got milked. I did that. That's character. I was born into it. Greatness is character before it's cash or cultural rank!"

I was born to greatness, though on a farm. It was there that I learned to take big risks. Yes, farmers spend hard-earned cash to buy seed, burying that seed in the ground and hoping to God that the rains come (and that the sun won't be too hot, and that the seeds will sprout and grow, and that the young plants won't be wiped out by hail or tornado). Farmers hope that they'll see grain and fruit on vine, branch, stalk, and stem.

Yes, I was born to greatness. I was born to a family that prayed together at all of our meals. And we read the Bible every day and went to church every Sunday. So I was born to live near the soil and the soul! That's where possibility thinking emerges!

5. I believe in hope!

Yes! I believe that tomorrow will surely arrive—anyway.

Yes! I believe that positive changes are possible—more than I see or know.

Yes! I believe that I'm a person—not a bird or an animal. I can choose to create the changes I'd like to see. And I can manage and manipulate the changes I didn't choose. I'm a person! I'm a possibility thinker!

Yes! I believe that I can turn obstacles into opportunities; stumbling blocks into stepping stones; problems into creative possibilities; competitors into partners. I can make my frustrations fruitful. I can declare dividends from my difficulties. My mistakes can become my most trusted teachers. My failures can become the key to unlock new doors I've never seen or valued before.

Yes! I believe positive forces are at work

that will surprise me with good news. Later to-day, or perhaps tomorrow, or maybe next week, I'll encounter new forces that will become new sources to lead my adventure to the break-through it needs.

Yes! I believe God is still alive. He knows where I am and how I got here. He's way ahead of me, maneuvering in the silence and the shadows. He really cares. I trust Him. The al-ternative is an unthinkable, unacceptable men-tal attitude that's certain to lead me down a path of hopeless despair.

Yes! I'm addicted to hope. That's my deci-sion. My hopes may not be completely ful-filled, but at least they're keeping me alive and alert and pragmatic. Hope promises to generate and sustain life (and then does). Despair prom-ises to generate and deliver depression and death (and then does). I'd rather choose hope (an emotional reaction that promises life but can't guarantee that all of its promises will be fulfilled) than choose despair (an emotional re-action that guarantees that its promises of fail-ure and death will surely be kept!).

I cannot and will not choose to become an impossibility thinker, turning my back on pos-sibility thinking. I'm going to change from a wanna-be to a gonna-be!

6. So I believe in ME!

Let me introduce you to an Olympic gold medal–winning member of my church. Her name is Janet Evans. She won four gold medals when she was barely seventeen. She was a champion. When Janet was twenty-four, the summer before the 1996 Olympics, a teenager beat her. And after that defeat, a teenager beat her once again.

Then came the Indianapolis tryouts for the 1996 Olympics. "I'm going to try again," she said. Negative reporters shook their heads. And hosts of people said, "Janet is over the hill." But she went to Indianapolis.

How did she do it? In her head and heart were the words, "I am! I can! I will! I believe!"

Ten minutes before Janet Evans opened her title defense in the four-hundred-meter free-style, her coach, Mark Schubert, took her aside and said to her, "Janet, don't forget who you are and all you've accomplished." And thus fortified, she took her dive into the water. She made the headlines the next morning: "Still some life left in Evans!"

The papers reported, "One by one Janet Evans shot down her rivals like clay pigeons." She left the teenagers in her wake. Then she took aim at the critics who'd suggested that she'd be dead in the water at these trials.

Although Janet didn't win a gold medal in the '96 Olympics, she still holds three world records: the four-hundred-meter freestyle, the eight-hundred-meter freestyle, and the fifteen-hundred-meter freestyle.

"A lot of people said I was washed up after the summer," the four-time Olympic gold medalist said, after coming from behind to win the four-hundred-meter freestyle at the trials. "But I never stopped believing in myself."

I'm told by lots of people that there are only two things that you can be sure of. Negative thinkers name death and taxes. But I'm telling you, as a positive thinker, that the two things you can be sure of are that the sun will rise tomorrow morning and set again tomorrow night, and that what happens in between is up to you!

In *The Touch of the Invisible*, Norman Grubb writes, "The greatest lie that has been perpetrated in this century is the lie that God is far away. But He is here! He is there! He is everywhere!" What Grubb says is true! God is here! And He's putting feelings in your heart and mine. He's motivating and managing us. He's making us into believers!

I am!
....
somebody.
....
I can!
....
do something.
....
I will!
....
make it happen.
....
I believe!
....
I will succeed.
....

God is at work in this world. God is saving people. God is connecting with people.

Let me repeat it again: Faith isn't a farce. Faith is a FORCE!

U.S. Air Force Captain Scott O'Grady was shot down in the skies over Bosnia on June 2, 1995. For six agonizing days and nights he relied on his survival training, his cunning, and his deep, deep faith in God to evade capture and death. He never lost trust in God. Scott was in an F–16 plane flying over Bosnia in support of the United Nations' peacekeeping effort to enforce a no-fly zone. His difficult assignment was to make sure that no airplanes were dropping bombs on people on the ground. Meanwhile, he had to stay away from surface-to-air missile sites and anti-aircraft artillery. Scott was flying his plane in support of the lead plane, piloted by his friend Captain Wright. Suddenly, when the two planes were over rugged mountainous terrain, two missiles were shot into the air. The second missile hit Scott's plane.

The missile destroyed the entire airplane. Scott was engulfed in flames and had to eject. Captain Wright never saw Scott eject, however; nor did he see a parachute.

Three times over, Scott thought he was going to die. First, when the missile hit and exploded; second, when he suspected that the ejection seat would be nonfunctional because of the explosion; third, when he worried that the parachute had been burned when the flames surrounded him, licking his face and neck. Scott prayed when the missile hit: "Dear God, don't let me die." He prayed as he reached for the ejection handle: "I've lived a beautiful life, but I still have something to live for, something I haven't experienced in life that means more to me than anything. Please, dear God, don't let me die." Scott described his experience to my *Hour of Power* audience:

To my relief I heard the canopy depart and the ejection seat functioned. I felt a rush of air, and then I was looking down at the ground from over five miles above the earth. Cockpit debris and plane wreckage were flying all around me. I pulled the handle to deploy the parachute.

It took a long time (about twenty-five minutes) to land, and I saw people on the ground pulling up with their vehicles waiting to capture me as soon as I hit the ground.

I landed in a little clearing. I got out of

my parachute, grabbed my survival gear, and started to run. By the time they'd get to my parachute, hopefully I'd be twenty miles south. I ran about a hundred yards, and suddenly I felt the whole overwhelming situation come collapsing down on top of me. I don't know why, but something made me stop. I ducked underneath some low-lying branches and hid there.

For six days people walked within just five feet of me, every day hunting for me. I also had a helicopter chasing after me. But I just lay very still, very motionless. I didn't want to give away my position. Hunters are attracted to movement before they're attracted to the animal itself. I'd go to every painstaking detail to save my life. Because your life is a very, very precious thing when it's threatened, and sometimes you forget that. It's a beautiful gift that God gave us.

It was six days of praying. It was six days of delving into the relationship that I have with my faith with God. And it wasn't so much having faith as it was having trust in that faith. I had a survival pack, but the water was gone within the first three days. After that I had to find water, but I couldn't get up and walk around, so the water had to come to me. When it came, it came in the form of rain. I used a sponge to collect that rain, because it wasn't raining heavily, and I'd squeeze that into a bag and drink from it later. That was an answer to prayer.

The last day there I ran out of water. My hiding place became a mud hole. My feet were wet, so I took my socks off, and I squeezed the water out of my socks and I drank it. There wasn't much there, but I would do anything to continue to be able to live. It wasn't the best-tasting water I've ever had in my life, but it helped me.

I didn't eat much. I didn't know I was going to be there for six days, because you can survive six days without eating at all. I thought I might be there longer, so I ate some leaves and some grass and ants. It wasn't even a small salad. If you eat one ant, it doesn't exactly fill you up.

But I never gave up. I put away wishful thinking. I put away negative thinking, even though I was faced with a reality I didn't like. I never gave up, and neither did my Air Force commanders back at the air base. They didn't know I was alive, but they never gave up on me. The day they rescued me, Captain Hamford, on a mission over Bosnia, was returning to his base. It was about two o'clock in the morning. His fuel supply was low, but he told himself, "One of my friends might be out there, and he's not in a very good position. I'm going to do whatever I can to maybe find him." So for twenty more minutes he searched the area.

He kept calling on the radio, and I finally heard him that night. Meanwhile, I kept praying, "Dear God, just let somebody know that I'm alive." I turned on the radio again. Then I heard his voice, after six days of not hearing anybody! I said, "This is Basher five-two. I'm alive. I'm alive!" He said, "Copy that. Good to hear your voice!" Only five and a half hours later I was rescued, which is an experience I shall never forget.

I had six days of really exploring my relationship with God and praying consistently. Never before had I had six days where I did that twenty-four hours a day, without any worldly distractions. That's an amazing thing to say, even though I was in a place where I didn't have the right to live. I could feel people were praying for me. I wasn't praying alone. It wasn't a solo prayer. And it wasn't just from the United States of America. The prayers came from all over the world. Even though I was by myself, I was never alone.

Scott said that he was taught his faith as a young boy by a very positive-thinking Catholic teacher, who said the most important part of your life is your relationship with God. Scott had faith before his days in hiding, but that experience definitely fortified it. Scott was quick to tell our audience, "I've always considered my faith a very personal thing, something that I don't normally go out and express. But when I came back, the only thing I wanted to do was tell the entire world about what a beautiful experience I had and that it was God's love that got me through."

When something catastrophic threatens, don't move; just think. Trust God. Hang in there. Keep your eyes on your goal. The course must be stayed! It's time for you to make a decision to tap into the spiritual forces that are a reality all around you.

I received a letter some time ago from a member of our church. It tells of someone who delayed life's most important decision. She wrote:

The people who live next door to me are very intelligent, they're very successful, they're financially well off, and they're socially high up, but he doesn't believe in God. We tried to get them to come to church, but they've never come. Then something happened only a couple of weeks ago. He and his wife went to an Angels baseball game. And during the game he said, "Excuse me, I think I've got to get up." She didn't say anything; he walked out. He went out to the balcony to get a breath of air, because he wasn't feeling well. As he stood on that balcony, what did he see a mile away, high in the sky, but the ninety-foot glowing cross of the Tower of Hope of the Crystal Cathedral. But he would never come here; he was an atheist.

After a considerable number of minutes had passed, his wife went out and found him. "Are you all right?" she asked. He looked at her with tears in his eyes and said, "I'm all right now. I've found God, honey. I've found Him." The next day he died of a heart attack.

Don't wait that long! God is alive, whether you believe in Him or not. God loves you, whether you love yourself or not. God is waiting for you, whether you're looking for him or not. I invite you now to discover the following: "I am God's child. He has a plan for me. I'm going to find it."

Obstacles? Mountains? The course must be stayed! Delayed? Okay . . . but stayed!

You're a possibility thinker. It's time for me to repeat for your benefit the Possibility Thinkers' Creed. I've inscribed this creed in books and on gold medallions, and I've often used it in sermons. Now, at the age of seventy, I repeat it—with a slight but significant revision. Here it is:

When faced with a mountain
I will not quit!
I will keep on striving until I
Climb over
Find a pass through
Tunnel underneath
or simply stay
and
turn my
mountain into a miracle
with God's help.
Amen

Hang in there, and the trumpets will be played—for you!

Trumpets? Yes indeed. Winston Churchill planned his own funeral and filled it with the promise of Easter. He directed that after the benediction, a bugler high up in the dome of St. Paul's Cathedral would play taps. Immediately after the playing of taps, a second bugler, also in the dome, would play reveille, a call to get up in the morning.

VIII

THE TRUMPETS
WILL BE PLAYED

—⟞⟝—

"**L**adies and gentlemen," the captain announces. "We're about to arrive at our home port. It's been a great trip!"

Yes, it's been a great trip. How honored I've been to be your tour guide!

Yes, you'll soon be home!

You're home when you know you've been faithful to your life's mission!

You're home when you look into the heart of the God who got you started, who prepared you for the adventure by stocking your mind, heart, and spirit with the supplies you needed on your tour of duty—a tour that was sometimes dangerous and difficult, but also delightful!

When He launched you on this trip, He met you alone and shared His dream for a better world. He said, "I have a dream. I want you to take it—and make it! I can't do it without a human body like yours—a brain to think with, a heart to love people through, eyes to see, ears to hear, hands to grasp, feet to run!"

And He shared His dream with you and you alone!

"But it's impossible!" you blurted out impertinently.

"If you were doing it alone, yes," He answered, adding, "But you and I together can make it happen!"

Still you hesitated.

"Without you it will never come true," He whispered. That shocked you. He was expecting too much!

And as He searched your soul for the faith to follow Him, you heard yourself whispering in your secret self the words He had put into your mind: "If it's going to be, it's up to me!" With that one sentence, you became a responsible person.

Yes, God gave you the dream. He set up the opportunity. He unfolded the possibilities, and He challenged you to assume responsibility for your destiny.

Now you can see that He was always there.

He put a burning desire within you! Your passion was God's presence.

He opened doors! And when you were spinning off course, He made the midflight correction.

He closed doors and opened new ones. He connected you with good people. New faces and voices came bearing precious gifts of encouragement and enthusiasm, reviving the spark of a dying dream into a new flame and renewing your hopes, almost buried under the hot ash.

When resources were depleted, fresh fuel came from surprising sources to support, sustain, and save you.

When you thought the road was about to end—remember? It didn't end at the foot of that mountain. God turned what looked like the end into a bend. You kept walking and then saw that there was a pass leading through!

Now, as the trip ends, you can see you owe it all to Him!

But He made you do it seemingly on your own. He never gave you guarantees. He knew you had to come back with the big prize: faith. Faith in yourself. Faith in good people. Faith in God's promise, presence, and power to achieve what He caused you to believe! Now you can see why He caused you to whisper to yourself at the outset, "If it's going to be, it's up to me!"

Surprise! Yes, you're surprised at the party

waiting for you at the terminal. As you step onto the gangway, you see held above the waiting crowd a large poster with your name in big letters, along with the words "Welcome Home!"

Then you see your friends, your family, your neighbors—yes, your entire community— standing on tiptoes, eyes misty, smiles wide, arms waving. You're their hero. You've become their inspiration. You're the dreamer of a dream that came true!

Now you hear it. Music. Trumpets! You see several trumpeters standing at the edge of the welcoming party, raising their trumpets for you!

You shed happy tears because you see the true picture. These laughing, cheering, applauding friends and relatives have been strong, silent supporters standing in your shadow, encouraging you to go for it. Again and again and again and again you would have failed without them.

When you first dreamed your dream and uttered that holy whisper—"If it's going to be, it's up to me!"—they were there for you.

As you look into their eyes, you realize that a big mistake is being made at this celebration. For the trumpets are aimed at you!

Wait a minute! You wave one arm to catch the eye of the trumpeters; with your other arm you point toward the welcoming party, wanting the musicians to turn their trumpets toward your friends and family in celebration of the success that they made possible.

The trumpeters notice your gesture. They turn and play for the unsung heroes. The coach. The teacher. The preacher. The spouse. The friend. The good, the faithful, the simple souls who made you who you are. Those unseen persons have fulfilled their mission too! Play the trumpets for them—here, now!

History is the record of the great dreams of great dreamers coming true.

I love the Olympics. These games regularly gather together the greatest and most inspiring collection of possibility thinkers in the world.

I was fortunate enough to attend the opening Olympic ceremonies in Los Angeles in 1984 and in Seoul, Korea, in 1988. In Seoul, I was surprised and delighted to meet up with my friend Andrew Young—then mayor of Atlanta, Georgia. We walked back to the hotel together.

"What brings you here, Andy?" I asked.

"I have a dream, Bob. I'd like to see the Olympics in the United States in 1996, and my dream is to get Atlanta accepted by the International Olympic Committee as the host city." His eyes flashed with passion, as if to say, "If it's going to be, it's up to me!" And Andrew Young pulled off his dream.

My friend David Foster was commissioned to write an inspirational song to be sung at the opening ceremonies in Atlanta in 1996. Two weeks before the games were to begin, he was back at the Crystal Cathedral to introduce the words and music on our national television program, *The Hour of Power.* His gifted wife, Linda Thompson, and Kenny Edwards contributed to the lyrics of his composition:

The Power of a Dream

Deep within each heart there lies a
   magic spark
That lights the fire of our imagination
And since the dawn of man, the strength
   of just "I can"
Has brought together people of all
   nations

There's nothing ordinary in the living of
   each day

There's a special part that every one of
   us will play

Feel the flame forever burn
Teaching lessons we must learn
To bring us closer to the power of the dream
The world unites in hope and peace
Pray that it will always be
It is the power of the dream that brings
   us here

There's so much strength in all of us
Every woman, child, and man
The moment that you think you can't
You'll discover that you can

It's the power of the dream
that brings faith in things unseen
Courage to embrace your fear
No matter where you are
Reach for your own star
To realize the power of the dream

One day David Foster called me up with a
fantastic invitation: "Dr. Schuller, how would
you and Mrs. Schuller like to go to the Olympics for the opening ceremonies? The best tick-
ets are selling for over six hundred dollars—but

I've got two for you. And you can fly out there as my guests on the plane I'm taking."

Wow! "With you playing your song and leading the music in that jam-packed stadium with fifteen thousand Olympians filling the field?" I exclaimed. "Gosh, David, how can I thank you?"

Then a tough call came—only two days before our plane was to leave. The news: "Dr. Beckering died." I cried and cried.

Then another call. This time Dr. Beckering's son. "Would you fly out to Michigan to preach at Dad's funeral?" he asked. "It will be on Saturday."

That would conflict with the Olympic opening ceremonies. Still, immediately I promised his son, "I'll be there."

Priorities were swayed. It was an easy decision. Dr. Beckering's funeral would be my greatest honor, for now I could tell the world how much of my entire ministry I owed to him. I was only twenty-three years old and a fresh graduate from Western Theological Seminary when the president of that institution telephoned Dr. Beckering.

Ray often reminded me what the president's instructions had been: "We've just graduated a young man named Robert Schuller. I think that he has real potential. We've given him the best formal education. He has to come under your wise guidance as he starts his career. Take him under your wings and shape him."

So Dr. Beckering presided over my ordination. He coached me. He managed me. He led the campaign in 1955 to nominate me to be elected as the minister who would be given the opportunity to start a new church in Garden Grove, California.

The rest is history. Years later, during the rapid growth of that church, I called Dr. Beckering to join me on staff, and I challenged him to organize and launch the New Hope crisis-intervention telephone center—the first in the United States to be staffed around the clock. As I mentioned in an earlier chapter, that center is housed in the Neutra-designed Tower of Hope. Dr. Beckering accepted my challenge. And he delivered. That was over twenty-five years ago.

It was time for me to blow the trumpets for Dr. Beckering. I arrived at my Grand Rapids, Michigan, hotel at nine o'clock on Friday night. I rushed to turn on the TV, determined to watch the live telecast of the opening ceremonies from Atlanta. Until midnight the celebration went on.

"And now, ladies and gentlemen, the torch is arriving in the stadium! It will be carried around the track and handed to the person who has been chosen as the last athlete to carry the flame, which came from Athens, Greece, to America. From California it's been carried by runners on foot all the way to Georgia. It's now outside the stadium. Who has been chosen to carry it for its last run? This runner will put it into the hands of Muhammad Ali, who will receive the flame to light the torch that will burn high in the sky for the entire Olympics."

From out of the crowd of fifteen thousand dedicated, disciplined winning Olympians emerged the person picked to be the last runner of the flame.

Then a name was called out: "Janet Evans!" The television camera came in close. And I cried and cried and cried. I hadn't known. No one had known. It was the best-kept secret of the Olympics. How beautifully she ran, holding the torch and flame high and bright! How strongly she ran! How radiant her smile! A member of my church! I wiped away my tears, put my hands to my lips, and alone (and loudly) "blew the trumpet" for Janet Evans! The next day I blew the trumpet again at the funeral of my colleague and hero, Dr. Beckering.

If it's going to be, it's up to me! Trumpets will continue to be played for Heather Whitestone Miss America 1995 too! Heather and I first met each other through a telephone call on her sixteenth birthday. Heather is one of three children. At the age of eighteen months she became ill with a virus. The doctor administered a drug that saved Heather's life but left her profoundly deaf. Little Heather Whitestone had to learn how to live a normal life despite her hearing loss.

As Heather approached her sixteenth birthday, her sister and brother-in-law, who were volunteers at the Crystal Cathedral, asked me to telephone Heather to wish her a happy birthday. (They explained that they had a special device to allow Heather to receive telephone calls.) Heather grew up watching our television program through closed captioning. (We were one of the first closed-captioned TV programs in the United States.)

Heather was enthusiastic: "When my mother said you telephoned, I thought you were Granddaddy. 'Heather, it's really Robert Schuller,' she said. You made my day! *The Hour of Power* is one of my favorite TV shows on Sunday. You inspire me a lot."

Heather has tackled unbelievable challenges since I've known her, including two attempts to become Miss America.

Heather told me that there were times during her first attempt at the title when she got discouraged and thought about quitting. After all, no totally deaf person had ever made it to the Miss America finals before. At least eighty thousand women compete for the title each year, starting with local competitions and moving on to regional and state events. Perhaps she should simply be grateful to have gotten this far—and call it quits. But deep down inside there was a God-inspired passion to try a second time.

On her second try, she again made it to Atlantic City. She remembered that she had found her first interview with the judges particularly challenging. Some of them couldn't understand all of her words. So this second time she introduced herself with just a few brave and inspiring words:

"When I was eighteen months old, I became very ill. The medicine given to me to save my life left me profoundly deaf. My mother was told that a normal life for me would be impossible. For example, I would never drive a car or go to a public school. But thank goodness, the word "impossible" is not in my family's vocabulary. On Wednesday night you'll see the result of believing in your dream; that's when I dance. And now it's my turn to take all my wishful thinking and energy to bring about my dreams. I want to be Miss America. I want to graduate from college. But I know each of you has a question: 'Can a profoundly deaf woman fulfill the duties of Miss Alabama and Miss America?' To this, I answer yes, I can do it. Because I realize that everything is possible with God's help. I don't see my deafness as an obstacle, but as an opportunity for creativity.

"I created the STAR program for elementary school children because I've seen so many young people during my high school and college years who've given up their dream too fast. I really believe God has very special dreams for each of us, so I help those kids to become a STAR. A STAR has five points: (1) a positive attitude, (2) a dream, and a willingness to (3) work hard, (4) face your problems, and (5) believe that with God's help anything is possible and one person can make a difference.

"I want you to know that when you ask me a question, I won't hear it. I'm deaf. I'll have to read your lips. But lip-reading at its very best will give me only about fifty percent of what you say. So I may repeat the question just to make sure I understand, or I may ask you to write it down to save time. But I'm excited about being here."

Then Heather told me that the judges' eyes were so big and friendly she knew she had won their hearts. I asked Heather what went through her mind when she heard her name called out as Miss America—not number three, not number two, not runner-up. But Miss America! What happened inside her ? How did she feel?

"I couldn't hear the announcement, but I was looking at a TV monitor and I could see the first runner-up. So I thought, 'Okay, well if she cries, then she won. If she doesn't cry, then I won.' And she didn't cry! I won! I was so excited. I walked down the runway and looked at all the people gathered there, and I said, 'Lord, I have a lot of things to do as Miss America, so You'd better come with me.' I learned a lot from Him during my year as Miss America. I learned that life is short. That I need to enjoy life fully. The things I have—my clothes, car, house—don't really make me happy. I learned not to work so hard. To try to enjoy my life and be grateful to God. Jesus became my Savior, and that's all I need!"

"But how can a profoundly deaf person dance when she can't hear the music?" I asked

350

her. "I hear it through the vibrations I feel," she answered. Heather came to dance as a professional in our Glory of Christmas celebration at the Crystal Cathedral, and her artistry moved people to tears.

Yes, the trumpets will be played for the winners, the overcomers, the bouncebackers, the truly penitent, the celebrities in the limelight, and the winning teammates who stand steadily as the silent encouragers in the shadows.

I first met Bill McGee in Moscow four years ago in the ambassador's office. Bill, originally a dentist by profession, went on for further schooling and specialization, earning his medical degree and becoming a plastic surgeon. He was one of twelve children, and he has five children of his own.

About ten years ago God really pulled a surprise on him. Bill, with his wife, was invited to go on a trip to the Philippine Islands to learn more about plastic surgery for children with cleft lip and cleft palate. When he arrived at the small clinic, he saw almost three hundred children with gaping holes in their lips who couldn't even talk. Their parents were pushing at the door and forcing their way in to say,

"Please, won't you take care of my child?"

"The team that we were with had time to take care of only about forty children," Bill said, "and so we watched two hundred and fifty children get sent home without any attention whatsoever. We felt so badly that the next year we went back and took care of about one hundred children, but we had to watch another two hundred and fifty children get sent home. We started to realize that we had the incredible opportunity to change the life of a child who was never going to be able to whistle or feel the gentleness of a kiss. We realized that in a forty-five-minute surgery we could create the miracle of a smile on the face of a child. A mother came to me with a little basket of bananas and tried to say, 'Thank you for changing the life of my child.'"

And so in 1982 Bill McGee said, "If it's going to be, it's up to me!" And Bill, along with his wife, organized Operation Smile. Plastic surgeons, nurses, dentists, and pediatricians now volunteer two weeks a year to join a team of thirty-five to forty-five professionals who travel around the world visiting over twenty-two different sites, giving a smile to children who are disfigured. There are millions of children who are hidden from their society—in the Philippines, Kenya, Colombia and other South American countries, and Vietnam. The members of Bill McGee's team have completed over seventy-five hundred of these Operation Smile surgeries. Bill is a dedicated Christian who has given his life to make this a better world! Bill's passion and dedication are evident as he tells about the "privilege" of changing a child's life.

President Reagan and President Bush both bestowed special awards upon Bill McGee, and I blow the trumpet loud and long for him, his wife, and Operation Smile. And in 1996 Operation Smile won the first humanitarian award of the year that carried a million-dollar prize! Bill McGee was only an average student, but he's summa cum laude when it comes to heart and soul!

Yes, the trumpets will be played for the cum laude students, but they'll also be played for those whose only A was for effort. You'll hear a fanfare for people in the lower ranks who (though their gifts and potential didn't match the valedictorians') never, never walked away, who hung in there and won the big prize.

The tassel was worth the hassle.

The trumpets will be played! They've played already for Herschel Walker, one of the greatest football players of all time. In 1992 Herschel received the Heisman Trophy. He keeps his body in condition by doing two thousand sit-ups, fifteen hundred push-ups, and fifty dips daily. He has only 1.42 percent body fat. He lives with the motto he learned from his mother: "Be the very best you can be!" So Herschel plays the trumpet for his mom.

"What was the secret of your success?" I asked this friend.

"Pray. Work. Go for it. Get in there and believe! You've got to buy your ticket. Then do it! That's the way everyone who succeeds makes it. But my special secret? My mom! She made a believer out of me. I had a speech impediment. 'You'll be okay,' she promised. And I'm a public speaker today. 'Believe in yourself; God does!' And every Sunday she'd take me and the other kids to church. I remember one Sunday I didn't want to go. I had only one pair of shoes. So I hid them and said, 'Mom, I can't go to church today. I lost my shoes.' She came smiling her command: 'Can't find your shoes, Herschel? God don't care if you don't wear shoes. Come anyway.' I did, and I'll never know how that really made me into the character I have become."

Herschel decided at the age of twelve to

dedicate his life to Jesus Christ, and he speaks openly about his faith to anyone and everyone.

Yes, the trumpets will be played for all great mothers. The trumpets will be played for all the homemakers—those who make the house a home and create a family in a fortress of faith for their children . . . children who now may be grown, standing in honor on stage to receive their hard-earned accolades. And they'll be played for the caregivers who keep the candles of loving faith burning in the dark days and nights.

I continue to play the trumpet for my mother. She was the oldest daughter born to an Iowa farm family that emigrated from the Netherlands. She was bright—really brilliant, in fact. But she was never given a chance to get a high school or college education because she was a girl. Her brothers were sent to college. But she was told, "Your role is to be a housewife and mother."

"Every person should strive to be the best at something," she believed. So that was her dream.

What was that? She was the best baker of apple pies in Alton, Iowa. Every time there was a funeral she'd pull one of her famous apple pies from her oven and have one of us kids take it to the grieving family. When it was my turn, I'd carry the huge apple pie carefully. The juice that leaked from the deep pie would be marbleized with melting cinnamon. I'd knock on the door.

"Mom wants you to know we're all praying for you," I'd say as I held out the apple pie fresh from my mom's oven. Hands of the grieving family reached out to take the gift from the hands and heart of my mom—a champion among the human spirits living in that small, simple Iowa town. My mom was the best at something. She knew it. I think she can hear the trumpets playing for her!

Why for her? For being the best at something, somewhere in the world. What's that? Baking apple pies in Alton, Iowa. Yes, but she was the best at something else that was far more important to me. She was the best mother in the world in my childhood family!

The trumpets were played for Aunt Hannah as well. The late Dr. William Stidger, one of my favorite inspirational ministers, tells of a sociology class from Johns Hopkins University that made a scientific study of one of the worst slums of Baltimore. The results unpromising, their report was filed in the archives of the university. The study's findings were tabulated on two hundred cards marked, "Headed for Jail." On each card was described a little rough urchin whose background, attitude toward life, and prospects strongly indicated that this person was headed for jail.

Twenty-five years later another sociology class found this report; they read about the two hundred kids—black and white kids, boys and girls—who were headed for jail. They decided to pursue every card and see what had actually happened to these young people. The first card they investigated led them to a prominent physician in Baltimore. They went to him and said, "You were described twenty-five years ago as an incorrigible kid headed for jail. How come you never got there?"

"It's true," the man admitted. "I was the worst kid in the neighborhood, but Aunt Hannah changed all that."

"Who's Aunt Hannah?" the students asked.

He explained that Aunt Hannah had been a teacher in the slums. One day she'd invited this youngster to her house for Sunday dinner. "Look, Joe," she told him, "I've been studying you, and I've discovered something in you that I want to tell you about. You have the capacity to be a terrific surgeon. I foresee the time when you'll be one of the greatest men in medicine in the city of Baltimore. I'm going to follow you, Joe, all the way."

"I walked out of Aunt Hannah's house," Joe said, "feeling that I couldn't let her down. 'She sees me as a great surgeon,' I remember saying to myself. 'What do you know! What do you know!' So I missed jail because of Aunt Hannah."

The study group went to another name on the list of incorrigibles; he too was now a grown man, the owner and manager of a beautiful supermarket. "You're on the list of youngsters expected to go bad," the students told him. "How come you're not in jail?"

He told them his story:

"I worked in a small grocery store that was on this very plot of ground. I used to steal stuff from that store where I worked and give it to my gang. I was a provider of food, and I stole it all. Of course, I finally got caught, but luckily I had enough sense to talk to Aunt Hannah. She didn't preach at me, but pointed out that when we do something wrong we must pay for it in some way. Was I willing to pay back all that I had stolen? I said I was. Aunt Hannah then worked it out with the grocer and the police.

"I worked in that grocery store and paid all

the money back. I liked working there. One day Aunt Hannah said to me, 'You're going to run one of the biggest and best grocery stores in Baltimore. What do you think?' She believed in me and helped me believe in myself. Finally I bought that very store and gradually improved and enlarged it into this supermarket. So this is the very site where I stole food and was headed for jail. But Aunt Hannah changed all that."

The trumpets are being played today for one of the world's foremost pioneering transplant surgeons, Dr. John S. Najarian. From his base at the University of Minnesota, where for years he was an esteemed professor of surgery, he developed a drug to help transplant patients to survive. Dr. Najarian perfected the drug and pressed on to acquire a license to produce and distribute it. That drug was a great success, and so was he. Lives were saved—and millions of dollars earned.

Part of that money was spent in transporting Dr. Najarian and his nurse-wife of over forty years on trips around the world, where he shared his skills at surgery. These funds came not from the university's revenue stream but from Dr. Najarian's profits from the development of his new drug. For some unknown reason, however, Dr. Najarian's expenditures caused suspicion in the University of Minnesota's administration. That suspicion escalated into acrimony and charges. Then lawyers (hired by the university but connected to federal authorities) indicted Dr. Najarian on fifteen counts. The Minnesota media churned these events into a horrific experience for one of that state's most honored and heroic persons.

When the two-year ordeal finally culminated in a verdict, Dr. Najarian was acquitted on every one of the fifteen counts, and a federal judge said that the case should never have gone as far as it did. When I heard about Najarian's acquittal, I wrote a congratulatory note to my dear friend. Here was his reply:

Thank you so much for your very kind letter regarding my acquittal on all counts and complete vindication for me.

My wife, Mignette, and I have enjoyed your current series on possibility thinkers. It reminded me so much of what transpired in our own lives recently.

As part of the investigation the federal government and the combined lawyers confiscated two million documents relating to all the correspondence, hospital records, patient records, financial records, etc., of our transplant program dating back over twenty-five years. The daunting task that I faced was how could we retrieve and make sense of these documents so that my attorneys would have a reasonable chance of defending me against this massive prosecution attack in the upcoming trial.

This is where the real possibility thinking began. My wife, Mignette, and her three sisters, all of whom readily admitted to being computer-illiterate (and I must admit, so was I, at that time), rented computers and laser printers that filled our entire living room in order to collate, categorize, and generally make a database of well over a million and a half pieces of paper, reading through five hundred and eighty-seven boxes of federal files, looking for information and putting it into the database. Never once did Mignette and her sisters waiver. With prayer and hard work they educated themselves to the point where they could accomplish this task, becoming computer wizards and presenting well-organized witness files in three-ring binders for my attorneys to peruse and use for my defense. These four women represented the absolute personification of possibility thinkers working every day, seven days a week, . . . from April 15, 1995, to January of 1996.

It was a sight to behold. When they weren't working, they were praying. I received so many letters, phone calls, and personal comments from patients, colleagues, faculty members, and total strangers who supported me and were praying for me. I had been fortunate to do a transplant surgery on a Catholic sister from the Contemplative Sisters of the Good Shepherd in Shoreview, Minnesota, and the entire sisterhood was praying for me as well. The power of prayer is an absolutely magnificent gift that God has given us all, and it works.

It certainly worked for Dr. Najarian. After months of agony he, his wife, and his family were gathered in the courtroom to hear the verdict. "Count one, dismissed," the judge announced. "Counts two, three, four, five, six, seven, eight, nine, ten, eleven, twelve, thirteen, fourteen, and fifteen . . . all dismissed," the judge ruled. Possibility thinking prevailed!

Possibilities were weighed.
Priorities were swayed.
Plans were laid.
Commitments were made.
The price was paid.
The timing was delayed.
The course was stayed.
And now, as promised, the trumpets were played!

The trumpets will be played for the honorable entrepreneurs. You'll find all colors and cultures in this heroic collection of possibility thinkers.

The trumpets may be played for some losers too! Does that include you? Are you facing a real setback? Bankruptcy? Divorce? Drug addiction? Prison?

You too can be rescued, renewed, revived, regenerated, restored, and respected!

Adversity? Admit it. Face it: that's your responsibility. Denial of negative reality is always a great danger. Addressing that danger is your department. Be your own best friend by moving from defense to offense. Alcoholics Anonymous begins here: "I need help; I cannot do it alone."

Confession is the most essential liberating step in the process of recovery.

"The adversity may or may not be your fault, but it's your responsibility now to pull out of it," my friend Richard DeVos wisely advises.

Put a positive spin on your predicament. You'll be a different person by the time your dark days pass. The future will be a better place if you become a better person because of your predicament.

How can adversity change you for the better? Look at who and where you are and where you want to go. Learn. You've made mistakes. Every single human has; no person is perfect. Lean on the best counsel you can find. Be genuinely humble. Lift others. All around you today—and in all of your tomorrows—there are human beings who are in bad straits. Turn your scars into stars. Teach others what you've learned the hard way.

Look at what others have done and how they've bounced back. I call the characteristic of resilience bouncebackability. I'm watching one of my dear friends, Stew Leonard, to see how he'll bounce back. He became a national celebrity by creating the world's largest —and best—dairy store in Connecticut. He was—and still is—one of the most inspiring persons I've ever met anywhere in the world. I've never been more shocked than when I learned that he'd been arrested. He confessed openly to the charge: he had for years been skimming cash from the company he owned to avoid reporting it as taxable income. He was sentenced to several years in a federal prison. He's still there as I write these lines.

Hardly had he arrived in prison when he was called to the warden's office. The warden locked eyes with Stew and said, "Mr. Leonard, what are you doing here? Why, you're a man I've admired so much! Once a week I'd drive seventy miles to your store to shop. You've been my hero. Why are you here?"

"I'm here, sir, because I broke the law," Stew admitted, "and I got caught. I'm here to pay the penalty I truly deserve."

When Stew needed an extensive medical checkup, he was allowed to go home for tests. Hearing he was on a short leave, I called him on his private home telephone number. The phone rang—once, twice, three times.

"Hello?" a voice said tentatively. I recognized that voice.

"Stew, this is the day the Lord has made. Let us rejoice and be glad in it."

Silence. Then, three thousand miles away, he exclaimed, "Oh, my God. It's Dr. Schuller. Oh, God; it's Bob. Oh, God!"

I could hear him beginning to cry, but I had to ask a tough question. "How, Stew? How could you have done that? You of all people?"

"Dr. Schuller, I can't tell you now. But when I'm out of prison I can talk, and I want to. I want to tell the world how it happened, and how it can happen to anyone. I have a terribly important story to tell, which I hope can save a lot of people out there from making what would be the biggest mistake of their lives."

I predict that the trumpets will play again for Stew Leonard.

Yes, the trumpets will play for the truly repentant soul. That's the heart of the gospel of Jesus Christ: "God so loved the world that He gave His only son that whosoever believes in Him shall not perish, but shall have eternal life" (John 3:16).

This is the story of the Bible. In its illuminating pages you meet the great people of inspiring faith. And of all the prophets, saints, and disciples, there's only one person whom God calls "a man after my own heart" (Acts 13:22). His name is David. He was not only king of Israel; he was the inspiring author of the hope-filled Psalms. He wrote Psalm 23—

poetry unsurpassed through the ages!

"The Lord is my shepherd." Those are the opening words. The closing words: "Surely, goodness and mercy shall follow me all the days of my life and I shall dwell in the house of the Lord forever."

But the David who wrote Psalm 23 also wrote Psalm 51. This short psalm is the classic confession of a truly positive penitent person. It was written after he'd committed adultery and then deliberately assigned the woman's husband to the front lines, where he was killed by the enemy.

From that sordid scene David went into the depths of sorrow and met the God who was willing to forgive him, an undeserving sinner. David experienced the grace of God. He experienced divine mercy: love in action for those who don't deserve it. No one ever really loves God as sincerely and deeply and profoundly as the person who's experienced that divine grace.

So no one is more beloved of God than the truly penitent soul.

And when God forgives us, he doesn't just establish us on the lower rungs of His ladder. He pardons us and puts us at the top of the ladder, where His beloved sons and daughters are honored!

The trumpets will be played for the soul that's been saved from the shame of sin. Check out the persons held up as the all-time spiritual heroes:

DAVID. "A man after my own heart."

ST. PETER. "On this rock I will build my church" (Matthew 16:18), Jesus promised as he looked into this penitent, precious soul. This same Peter would deny his Lord when Jesus was on trial.

ST. PAUL. No person was more powerful in bringing Christianity to the whole world than this man. But didn't St. Paul literally kill many of the first Christians? Yes, but he—like David and Peter—changed.

These penitent sinners were literally, spiritually born again—out of shame into glory. Listen to the trumpets played for them by the angels in heaven.

Now let me share a very personal story with you, an awesome experience I'm going through as I close this book. I was never at the top of my class during my four years at Hope College. How shocked I was—many years ago—to receive the two highest honors that school could offer an alumnus. First I was surprised to receive an honorary doctor of divinity degree. Then I was given a second honor, one more important to me than the first: the distinguished alumnus award. During all my college years I struggled with grades in full-time classes while working odd jobs to pay my college bills. To be so richly honored years later was a deeply humbling experience. It made me feel good to know that those who'd trusted me before I proved worthy of their faith could see my progress and be proud of what I'd done and become.

After college I enrolled, as I've mentioned, at Western Theological Seminary—a three-year postgraduate school in Holland, Michigan. I did well there: I graduated with honors and was ordained. In California I started a church in a drive-in theater. That move wasn't looked upon with respect by either my denomination or my seminary. In fact, I embarrassed both. When I launched the self-esteem movement in Christianity, I was viewed with real suspicion. When I began televising church services and created the first national television church in America, there were increasing whispers about me in the shadows. My books were criticized at the seminary as pop psychology—"shallow theology," the professors said. My books, I was told, weren't promoted for sale in the seminary bookstore where students could buy them. Many letters—and more than one book—were written to attack me as a theologian with a distorted gospel.

Then some years ago the leading daily newspaper in western Michigan came out with a major story on me, using quotes from professors at my own seminary who faulted my sermons as "shallow" and my attitude toward sin as "cavalier." One quote from a theology professor used the adjective "demonic."

I was out. Boy, was I! I was never ever—not once—asked by these theological critics to comment on their criticisms before they were published. No graduate of that hundred-year-old theological school had ever been so exposed in a major secular news story as I was to what I saw as unfair interpretations. And I didn't know about their criticisms until I read them in the secular media! Apparently my life's work continued to be a source of embarrassment to my respected postgraduate school of religion.

Wonderful honors came to me, however,

from other sources. In 1991 the government of the Netherlands honored me by naming a new tulip after me—in the four-hundredth anniversary year of the tulip. In 1996 the city of Holland, Michigan, offered an invitation to me to be the grand marshal of the 1997 Tulip Parade.

Then the letter came from the president of my theological seminary, the graduate school whose leading professors had so sharply criticized me for so many years. With the passing of years the professors had changed—surely, slowly, carefully, and prayerfully.

I read his letter, alone and quietly, as I celebrated my seventieth birthday:

Dr. Schuller: As president of Western Theological Seminary it is my honor to tell you that Western Theological Seminary invites you—when you come to Holland in 1997 to lead the Tulip Parade—to visit your seminary and deliver a lecture to the entire faculty and students. And on this occasion you have been chosen to receive from the seminary the first Distinguished Alumni Award ever offered in the history of this school.

I cried and I thought I heard—far off in the distance—the sound of a trumpet. Then I read again a poem I'd written in the hurtful years based on the Bible text:

"And the time of the singing
of the birds has come . . ."
Song of Solomon, 2:12

When
the night is past
and
the dawning of a new day
is
about to break
with
fresh hopes and dreams,
then
you will hear . . .
the singing of the birds.

When
storm clouds break
to drift away
leaving bright patches of blue
with golden shafts of sunlight
on
flower and leaf

sparkling with fresh drops of diamond
  rain,
then
you will hear . . .
the singing of the birds.

Yes
there are those times and places
when
the cold winter ends
Springtime returns.
The dark night of the soul
is dissolved in a happy daybreak.
The storm is over.
Then
you will hear . . .
the singing of the birds.

Yes! The trumpets will be played!

That's my experience. When I celebrated my seventieth birthday, friends and family gathered from across America. In the course of the evening, toasts were offered. Carol, my daughter, now married and a mother of four children, rose and said, "I want to read a poem I wrote today for my father." She read these words to eyes filling with tears throughout the great hall.

The Dreamer

The dreamer looked, no, gazed, upon
What he did not know
And as he looked and gazed therein
He saw a distant glow
Of something that could be
From something that was not.
And as that glow grew great and grand
The Dreamer stretched his youthful hand,
To touch the "What-Could-Be"
And suddenly the glow became
The heart of "What-Is-He."
And then the Dreamer dreamed again
And then he dreamed again.
Through months and days and years,
Through joy and pain and tears,
Through hope and doubt and fears.
And when the day became the dusk
His life set as the sun
And as the Dreamer dreamed his last,
His dreams had just begun.

Poem written by Carol Schuller Milner
Copyright © 1996
Used by permission

EPILOGUE

—⚍—

N ow—let's build a better world!
Join me at an afternoon assembly of
the American Academy of Achievement
in June 1996. On stage a distinguished panel is
addressing this subject: "Can we build a better
world?" Listening are our guests—over three
hundred of the brightest high school seniors
from all fifty of the United States of America.

Join me: drop in and listen, as I am listening, to a small collection of possibility thinkers discussing that sobering question. Larry
King, television talkshow host; Willie Brown,
mayor of San Francisco; Elie Wiesel, humanitarian and Nobel Peace Prize winner; Johnetta
B. Cole, president of Spelman College; and
Craig McCaw, a major player in the development of cellular telephones. These are the distinguished panelists.

The thoughts and words are flying! Sentences sometimes come and go faster than I can

connect them to the panelists. *Who said that?* Here's just a small portion of what's being said:

VOICE ONE: "We in today and tomorrow's information age are more powerful than any kings ever were." Was that Craig McCaw's voice?

VOICE TWO: "Yes, we know more, but we care less."

VOICE THREE: "We're less human with what we do with our knowledge," Elie Wiesel responds.

VOICE FOUR: "Can we teach virtue? Without it the information age can lead to global anarchy."

ELIE WIESEL: "Only by example."

DR. COLE: "I'm really struck by the power of the individual."

SOMEONE INTERRUPTS: "Are we smiling pessimists or weeping optimists?"

LARRY KING, TURNING TO WILLIE BROWN: "Is it possible for minorities to be optimistic?"

WILLIE BROWN: "Is it possible for minorities to be optimistic?" Willie Brown repeats the question. Then he exclaims, "It's absolutely *necessary* for minorities to be optimists! Always! Look at me. I'm the end product of optimism. I was born black in the South when and where racism was really bad. In that place and time I wasn't eligible to go to college. I believed that somehow, somewhere, I could and would. And I did. Optimism is the only way to go when things are tough and rough."

Then Larry King faces the group and asks a loaded question: "What do we 'haves' owe to the 'have-nots'?"

They all answer the question with one word: "Hope!" Then someone adds, "Be optimistic; it's the only sensible choice."

That's what I pray these pages bring to your heart: hope.

Then, when you feel this passion stir, call the feeling by the right name: it's God stirring within you!

Follow the call of hope leading you down the narrow path that leads to life! Never leave that path. And I promise you, someday you'll hear the happy sound! The trumpets will be played! For you!

Amen and Hallelujah!

Look for these latest Walker Large Prints:

Just As I Am
Billy Graham

Finding God in Unexpected Places
Philip Yancey

Abiding in Christ
Cynthia Heald

15 Minutes Alone with God
Emilie Barnes

The Hiding Place
Corrie ten Boom

I've Got to Talk to Somebody, God
Marjorie Holmes

A Touch of His Freedom
Charles Stanley

Breakfast with Billy Graham

On the Anvil
Max Lucado

A Path Through Suffering
Elisabeth Elliot

A Touch of His Wisdom
Charles Stanley

Among the many other titles available are:

And the Angels Were Silent
Max Lucado

Apples of Gold
Jo Petty

The Best of Catherine Marshall
edited by Leonard LeSourd

A Book of Angels
Sophy Burnham

Book of Hours
Elizabeth Yates

Brush of an Angel's Wing
Charlie W. Shedd

Encourage Me
Charles Swindoll

Finding God
Larry Crabb

A Gathering of Hope
Helen Hayes

Getting Through the Night
Eugenia Price

God Came Near
Max Lucado

Golden Treasury of Psalms and Prayers
Edna Beilenson

Good Morning, Holy Spirit
Benny Hinn

The Grace Awakening
Charles Swindoll

The Greatest Salesman in the World
Og Mandino

The Greatest Story Ever Told
Fulton Oursler

The Guideposts Christmas Treasury

Heaven: Your Real Home
Joni Eareckson Tada

Hinds' Feet on High Places
Hannah Hurnard

Hope and Faith for Tough Times
Robert Schuller

Hope for the Troubled Heart
Billy Graham

I Am with You Always
G. Scott Sparrow

The Jesus I Never Knew
Philip Yancey

The Knowledge of the Holy
A. W. Tozer

Laugh Again
Charles Swindoll

Lord, Teach Me to Pray
Kay Arthur

More Than a Carpenter
Josh McDowell

No Wonder They Call Him the Savior
Max Lucado

The Power of Positive Thinking
Norman Vincent Peale

Prayers & Promises for Every Day
Corrie ten Boom

The Pursuit of Holiness
Jerry Bridges

Six Hours One Friday
Max Lucado

The Source of My Strength
Charles Stanley

Strength to Love
Martin Luther King Jr.

Three Steps Forwards, Two Steps Back
Charles Swindoll

To Help You Through the Hurting
Marjorie Holmes

To Mother With Love
Helen Steiner Rice

A Treasury of Christmas Classics

What Happens to Good People
When Back Things Happen
Robert A. Schuller

Where Is God When It Hurts
Philip Yancey

The Wonderful Spirit-Filled Life
Charles Stanley